RICHARD MABEY, author and editor of educational books, broadcasts frequently on TV and radio, and shares his time between Hertfordshire and a cottage in Suffolk. He is the author of *The Unofficial Countryside*, *The Roadside Wildlife Book*, and *The Pollution Handbook*, and is at work on a successor to *Food for Free* about the non-edible uses of British wild plants, and an edition for Penguin Classics of Gilbert White's *The Natural History of Selborne*. Mr Mabey is a patron of the Kenneth Allsop Memorial Trust.

Richard Mabey

Food for Free

with 8 colour plates
and 148 pen and ink drawings by

MARJORIE BLAMEY

FONTANA/COLLINS

First published by Wm Collins Sons & Co. Ltd, 1972
First issued in Fontana 1975

Copyright © Richard Mabey 1972

Set in Monotype Garamond
Made and printed in Great Britain by
William Collins Sons & Co. Ltd, Glasgow

FOR MY MOTHER

Contents

Colour Plates

6. Herbs

Marjoram; Tansy; Wild angelica; Borage; Wild basil; Ramsons; Corn mint; Woodruff; Wild celery; Sweet gale; Wild thyme; Fenugreek

7. Flowers and Spices

Broom; Poppy; Black mustard; Hardhead; Coriander; Heather; Elder; Wild rose, dog rose; Sweet Violet; Primrose; Common chamomile

8. Fruits

Snowberry; Rowan; Strawberry tree; Whitebeam; Barberry; Oregon grape; Guelder rose; Cloudberry; Sloe; Medlar; Rose hip; Hottentot fig

Introduction

The first time I was offered a whole dish of wild vegetables I was frankly scared. The plant was marsh samphire, a skinny little succulent that grows abundantly on saltings. It lay on my plate like a mound of shiny green pipecleaners, and I went through all the usual anxieties one experiences when confronted with an unfamiliar food. Couldn't the tradition of eating the stuff be a horrible mistake? Might it not contain cumulative poisons whose effects appeared years later, when the fateful meal was forgotten? Did my friend really know enough about shore plants to have picked the right species? To be embarking upon such a strange and risky eating venture seemed – dare I say it – *unnatural*. When caution was eventually abandoned for the sake of science, the taste, needless to say, was a revelation.

I have been through a number of years and many hundreds of wild foods since then. Yet, though the morbid worries have long vanished, I still sometimes experience this sense of engaging in an eccentric and slightly hazardous activity whenever I gather or eat wild plants. It is sad and not a little remarkable how thoroughly we are all constrained by modern attitudes to food. For all our superficial preferences for 'home-grown' produce, it is those foods that are grown farthest from our sight that seem to be the most popular. There must be no hint of the dirtiness or the ups and downs of the growing process. The produce must be attractive, shapely, regular – all the things that plants rarely are in the wild. The most natural-looking foods are the ones that seem least 'naturally' desirable. So not only are we cut off from samphire, and many other delectable wild foods, but from a first-hand knowledge of what food *is*, and how it gets to us.

This paradox is most marked in the modern supermarket, round whose fruit and vegetable sections I often used to stroll whilst writing this book, wondering gloomily if anyone could ever be persuaded to venture beyond those seductive shelves.

Their contents seemed to epitomise healthy modern living: clean, bright, bountiful and including probably half a dozen exotic varieties that were scarcely known ten years ago. Yet it is difficult to believe that some of these products actually *grow*, so perfect are their proportions.

It is easy to forget in these conditions that half of them are, somewhere, somebody's naturally-occurring weeds. So were all the rest a few centuries ago. Every single one of the world's vegetable foods was once a wild plant. What we buy and eat today is nothing more special that the results of generations of plant-breeding experiments. Most of these, understandably, were directed towards improving size and cropping ability. Some were concerned with flavour and texture – but these are fickle qualities, dependent for their popularity as much on fashion as on any inherent virtue. Lately there have been more ominous moves towards improving colour and shape. As with the breeding of animals, the improvement of specific qualities like these is likely to lead to the deterioration of others. In the case of fruits it is usually the flavour, as anyone who has been tempted by giant, brilliant scarlet tomatoes will know.

Yet if plant breeding has been directed towards the production of bland, inoffensive flavours, and has sacrificed much for the sake of convenience, those old robust tastes, those curly roots and fiddlesome leaves, are still there for those who care to seek them out. Almost every British garden vegetable (greenhouse species excepted) still has a wild ancestor flourishing here. Wild cabbages grow along the south coast, celery along the east. Wild parsnips flourish on waste ground everywhere. In times of scarcity they are turned to again, yet each time with less ingenuity and confidence, less native knowledge about what they are and how they can be used.

I wrote this book because it seemed sad to me that this enormous storehouse of free, wild food is now all but ignored, and that the ability to capitalise on it is in danger of vanishing from popular knowledge. Of course, there are a few exceptions. Many people gather nuts in the autumn, and almost everyone picks blackberries. A few brave souls even browse for wild mushrooms. But what else? There are at least 320 wild food products growing in this country (including shellfish, but excluding higher fish, birds, and mammals) 130 of which are common throughout the British Isles.

Food for Free is about these plants, and how they have and can still be used as food. It is a practical book, I hope, but not an urgent one. It would be foolish of me to pretend that there are any pressing economic reasons why we should have a large scale revival of wild food use. You would need to be a most determined picker to keep yourself alive on wild vegetables, and since they are so easy to cultivate there would be very little point in trying. Nor are wild fruits and vegetables necessarily more healthy and nutritious than cultivated varieties – though some are, and most of them are likely to be comparatively free of herbicides and other agricultural poisons.

Why bother then? Why not leave wild food utterly to the birds and slugs? My initial pleas are, I'm afraid, almost purely sensual and indulgent: interest, experience, and even, on a small scale, adventure. The history of wild food use is interesting enough in its own right, and those who would never dream of grubbing about on a damp woodland floor for their supper may still find themselves impressed by our ancestors' resourcefulness. But those who are prepared to venture out will find more substantial rewards. It is the flavours and textures that will astonish most, I think, and the realisation of just to what extent the cultivation and mass production of food have muted our taste experiences. There is a whole galaxy of powerful and surprising flavours preserved intact in the wild stock, that are quite untapped in cultivated foods: tart and smoky berries, strangely aromatic fungi, crisp and succulent shoreline plants.

There is much along these lines that could be said in favour of wild foods. Many of them are delicacies, most of them are still abundant, and all of them are free. (I was not going to make too much of this last point, but looking at the prices of those gleaming supermarket products, I wonder if I was right.) They require none of the rather tedious attention demanded by garden plants, and possess the additional attraction of having to be *found*. I think I would rate this as perhaps the most attractive single feature of wild food use. The satisfactions of cultivation are slow and measured. They are not at all like the excitement of raking through a rich bed of cockles, of suddenly discovering a clump of sweet cicely, of tracking down a bog myrtle by its smell alone. There is something akin to hunting here: the search, the gradually acquired wisdom about season and habitats, the satisfaction of having proved you can provide for yourself. What you find may make no more than an intriguing addition to your normal diet, but it was you that found it. And in coastal areas, in a good autumn, it could be a whole three-course meal!

Wild Food and Necessity
It is not easy to tell how wide a range of plants was eaten before agriculture began. The seeds of any number of species have been found in neolithic settlements, but these may have already been under a primitive system of cultivation. Plants gathered from the wild would inevitably drop their seed and begin to grow near their pickers' dwellings; and if, as was likely, the specimens collected were above average in size or yield, so might be their offspring. So a sort of automatic selection would have taken place, with crops of the more fruitful plants growing naturally near habitation.

By the Elizabethan era, the range of wild plants and herbs used and understood by the average housewife was wide and impressive. In many ways it had to be. There was no other source of readily available medicine and not a great number of cultivated vegetables. Yet even under conditions of necessity, how is one to explain the discovery that as cryptic a part as the *styles* of the saffron crocus were useful as a spice? The number of wild bits and pieces that must have been put to the test in the kitchen at one time or another is hair-raising. We should be thankful the job has been done for us.

Many plants passed into use as food at this time as a by-product of their medicinal use. Blackcurrants, for instance, were certainly used for throat lotions before the recipients realised they were also quite pleasant to eat when you were well. Sheer economy also played a part, as in finding a use for the hop tops that had to be thinned out in the spring.

But like so much else, these old skills and customs were eroded by industrialisation and the drift to the towns. The process was especially thorough in the case of wild foods because cultivation brought genuine advances in quality and abundance. But if the knowledge of how to use them was fading, the plants themselves continued to thrive. Most of them prospered as they had always done in woods and hedgerows. Those that flourished best in the company of man bade their time under fields which had been turned over to cultivation, or moved into the new wasteland habitats that were a by-product of urbanisation. Plants which had been introduced as pot-herbs clung on at the edges of gardens, as persistent as weeds as they were once abundant as vegetables.

Then some crisis would strike the conventional food supplies, and people would be thankful for this persistence. On the island fringes of Britain, where the ground is poor and the weather unpredictably hostile, the tough native plants were the only invariably successful crops. The knowledge of how to use these plants as emergency rations was kept right up to the time air transport provided a reliable lifeline to the mainland.

It was the two World Wars, and the disruptions of food supplies that accompanied them, that provided one of the most striking examples of the usefulness of wild foods. All over occupied Europe fungi were gathered from woods, and wild greens from bomb sites. In America, pilots were given instructions on how to live off the wild in case their planes were ditched over land. And in this country, the government encouraged the 'hedgerow harvest' (as they called one of their publications) as much as the growing of carrots. I have told later in the book the full story of the rose-hip campaign, which is probably the best known of these war-time efforts. In fact this was an off-shoot of the work of the National Herb Committees. These were chiefly concerned with collecting plants for the drug firms, and so are not strictly relevant to this book. But their story does illustrate some of the advantages of wild plant use – and indeed just what can be gathered if sufficient hands are mobilised.

Before the war something like 90 per cent of all the herbs that were used in the commercial drug industry were imported to this country. By 1940 almost the whole of the European and Far-eastern contribution to this trade was cut off, and the government realised that the country could face a serious shortage of vital drugs unless some effort was made to obtain the necessary plants from within our shores.

So, the Ministry of Health set up a structure of voluntary pickers under the County Herb Committees, and a crash programme of education in identification and gathering techniques was set in motion. During the five years of the war over 750 tons of *dried* herbs (probably something like 4000 tons of fresh) were gathered by the Herb Committees. Rutland alone collected 4 tons of Belladonna leaf. The Committees were also responsible for gathering rose-hips, nettles for camouflage dyes, and perhaps most importantly the gelatine-yielding seaweeds, *Gigartina stellata* and *Chondrus crispus* (see pp. 116-7). Without the large quantities of agar jelly derived from these seaweeds, the development of penicillin might have been seriously delayed.

Wild plants are invaluable during times of famine or crisis, precisely because they are wild. They are quickly available, tough, resilient, resistant to disease, indifferent for the most part to climate and soil condition. If they were not, they would have simply failed to survive. They are always there, waiting for their moment, thriving under conditions that our pampered cultivated plants would find intolerable.

Some modern agriculturalists are beginning to look seriously at these special qualities of wild food plants. Conventional agriculture works by taking an end food product as given, and modifying plants and conditions of growth to produce it as efficiently as possible. In regions that are vastly different from the plant's natural environment, its survival is always precarious, and often at damaging expense to the soil. The alternative approach is to study the plants that grow naturally and luxuriantly in the area, and see what possible food products can be obtained from them. This looks like being an especially fruitful line of research in developing countries with poor soils.

But we might even be able to gain something from this approach back home, The elder would be an ideal subject, growing as it will in almost any environment. Its flowers make wine, fritters and a flavouring for jellies, its berries make jams and sauces, and even its pith is used in the cutting of sections for microscopy.

Plant Use and Conservation

I have spent the last few pages talking about conditions in which wild food use was anything but a frivolous pastime. I sincerely hope that this book will never be needed as a manual for that sort of situation. But is there really nothing more to gathering wild foods than the fun of the hunt, and the promise of some exotic new flavours? I think there is. Getting to know these plants and the uses that have been made of them is to begin to understand a whole section of our social history. The plants are a museum in themselves, hangovers from times when palates were less fastidious, living records of famines and changing fashions and even whole peoples. To know their history is to understand how intricately food is bound up with the whole pattern of our social lives. It is easy to forget this by the supermarket shelf, where the food is instantly and effortlessly available, and soil and labour seem part of another existence. We take our food for granted as we do our air and water, and all three are threatened as a result.

Yet get to know the ways of just a few of the plants in this book and you will see at first hand the complex and delicate relationships which plants have with their environment; their dependance on birds to carry their seeds, animals to crop the grass that shuts out their light, on wind and sunshine and the balance of chemicals in the soil, and ultimately on our own good grace as to whether they survive at all. It is on the products, wild or cultivated, of this intricate network of forces that our very sustenance depends.

I know there may be some people who will object to this book on the grounds that it may encourage further depletions of our dwindling wild life. I believe that the exact opposite is true. One of the major problems in conservation today is not how to keep people *insulated* from nature but how to help them engage more closely with it, so that they can appreciate its value and vulnerability, and, most importantly, the way its needs can be reconciled with those of man. The most complex and intimate relationship which most of us can have with the natural environment is to eat it. I hope I am not overstating my case when I say that to personally follow this relationship through, from the search to the cooking pot, is a more practical lesson than most in the economics of the natural world. Far from encouraging rural vandalism, it helps deepen respect for the interdependence of all living things. At the very least it will provide a strong motive for looking after individual plants; no one is going to stand by whilst the hedge which provides his sloe gin is bulldozed down.

Food for Free

Omissions

This book covers the majority of wild food products which can be obtained in the British Isles. But there are some categories which I have deliberately omitted, and I should make a note of these here.

There is nothing on grasses and cereals.[1] This is intended to be a *practical* book, and no one is going to waste their time hand-gathering enough wild seeds to make flour.

I have touched briefly on the traditional herbal uses of many plants where this is relevant or interesting. But I have included no plants purely on the grounds of their presumed therapeutic value. This is a book about food, not medicine.

This is also a book about wild *plant* foods, which is the simple reason (apart from personal qualms) why there is nothing about fish and wildfowl. But I have included shellfish because from a picker's eye view, they are more like plants than animals. They are gathered, not caught. They stay more or less in one place, and the only equipment needed to pick them with is a bucket.

Some picking rules

I have given detailed notes on gathering techniques in the introductions to most of the individual sections (on fungi, fruit,

---

1. Though during that great time of invention and make-do, the Second World War, at least one person turned to grass itself. A commendable piece of enterprise, though most readers who have ever munched a blade or two themselves will take this lyrical description with more than a pinch of salt:

> ... By devoting attention to the careful drying of grass into hay, I have been able to so dry it artificially, that when I was eating my repast, consisting of hay with other ingredients, I appeared to myself to be eating the most delightful meal, which was pervaded by the taste and aroma of new-mown hay. In like manner, by cutting up and mixing with freshly cut grass mowings, the petals of roses, lettuce leaves, and fruit, and adding sugar to my taste, I have been able to make myself most delicious salads. I have also been able by adding cut-up rose leaves to make a salad which consisted of fresh grass, rolled oats, sugar, and half an ounce of currants, to produce a meal which gave me the sense that I was enjoying a repast which had the taste and the aroma of fresh leechees, an Eastern fruit of the most delicate and delicious flavour.
>
> J. R. B. Branson quoted in *They Can't Ration These*.

etc.). But there are some general rules which apply to all the entries in this book, and which may help guarantee the quality of what you are picking, and the health of the plant that is providing it.

Although we have tried to make both text and illustrations as helpful as possible in identifying the different plant products described in this book, they should not be regarded as a substitute for a comprehensive field guide. They will help you decide what to gather, but until you are experienced it is wise to double-check everything (particularly fungi) before eating in a book devoted solely to identification (some are mentioned in the book list on p. 187). Conversely, never rely on illustrations alone as a guide to edibility. Some of the plants illustrated here (e.g. guelder rose) need the special preparation described in the text before they are palatable.

But although it is obviously crucial to know what you are picking, don't become obsessed about the possible dangers of poisoning. This is a natural worry when you are trying wild foods for the first time (as I know only too well myself!) but happily a relatively groundless one. As you will see from the Appendix there are surprisingly few poisonous plants in Britain compared with the total number of plant species. Most of them, too, are uncommon.

To put the dangers of wild foods into perspective it is worth considering the trials attendant on eating the cultivated foods we stuff into our stomachs without question. Forgetting for a moment the perennial problems of additives and insecticide residues, how many people know that, in excess, cabbage can cause goitre and onions induce anaemia? That as little as one whole nutmeg can bring on days of terrifying hallucinations? Almost any food substance can occasionally bring on an allergic reaction in a susceptible subject, and oysters and strawberries have particularly infamous reputations in this respect. But all these effects are rare. The point I am making is that they are part of the hazards of eating itself, rather than of a particular category of food.

But if you do want to be doubly sure, it is as well to try fairly small portions of new foods the first time you eat them, just to ensure that you are not sensitive to them.

Having considered your own survival, consider the plant's. Never strip a plant of leaves, berries, or whatever part you are picking. Take small quantities from each specimen, so that its appearance and health are not affected. It helps to use a knife or scissors (except with fungi, see p. 39).

Never take the flowers or seeds of annual plants; they rely on them for survival.

Never pull up whole plants along any path or road verge where the public has access. It is not only anti-social and contrary to all the principles of conservation, but also, in most places, illegal.

It is unwise to gather any sorts of produce from areas that may have been sprayed with insecticide or weed killer. Avoid, too, the verges of heavily-used roads, where the plant may have been contaminated by car exhausts. There are plenty of environments that are likely to be comparatively free of all types of contamination: commons, woods, the hedges along footpaths, etc. Even in a small garden you are likely to be able to find something like twenty of the species described in this book.

Wherever possible use a flat open basket to gather your produce, to avoid squashing. If you are caught without a basket, and do not mind being folksy, pin together some dock or burdock leaves with thorns.

When you have got the crop home, wash it well, and sort out any old or decayed parts.

Layout of the Book

The book is divided up into sections that correspond to food types, e.g. shellfish, herbs, fruit. Inside each section I have given every entry a category rating of A, B or C.

A entries are common and good to eat and are treated in full.

B entries are also common and good to eat, but are given a nominal treatment because they bear close resemblance to the preceding A entry.

C entries are included mainly for historical interest. They consist of plants which have been used in the past, but which I cannot recommend now, either because they are rare, like the early purple orchis, or indifferent eating, like the great plantain. It should be clear from each entry why any given plant has been given this rating. Inside the C category there are also a few tentative entries (e.g. snowberry) which ought to be edible but about which I would welcome more information.

The plants with similar ratings inside any section are arranged in the order in which they occur in Collins Field Guides (see Book List) which I would recommend for verifying identifications.

Then follows a list of some of the plant's local names. The majority of these are taken from Geoffrey Grigson's *The Englishman's Flora*, a book I am indebted to in many ways. I have not tried to give comprehensive lists, but to select the most pervasive names, and in particular those which give some clue to the plant's taste or traditional use.

The notes on the plants' distributions are based on the *Atlas of the British Flora*.

The recipes in the larger entries come from an enormous range of sources, both first-hand and written. I would hope that, like the country cooks who devised them, readers of this book will not be afraid to experiment.

Acknowledgements

I should like to thank J. E. Manners and the publishers of *Country Life* for permission to quote an extract from 'Truffle Hunting In England'.

Many people helped and gave advice during the preparation of this book. I should like to thank especially the Secretary and library staff of the Royal Horticultural Society, R. J. Kiel of the Publications Branch, and the library staff of the Ministry of Agriculture, Fisheries and Food; also A. A. Forsyth, author of the Ministry's excellent booklet on British Poisonous Plants, who gave me invaluable advice on the edibility of some entries; and Miss Pamela North, of the Pharmaceutical Society of Great Britain.

I need hardly add that the final selection of entries and the judgments expressed upon them are completely my own.

Most of all I would like to thank the many friends who have tramped the countryside with me over the last few years, helping to find and pick the plants described in this book, and who have eaten, without a murmur, concoctions and objects they had never even heard of: Rose - who guided me round some of the the rich fastnesses of North Norfolk - David, Drew, Ian, Nic and Sue, Mouse and Alan, Peter and Deedee, and Marian Newbold, who also retyped my dauntingly scruffy manuscript.

Shellfish

It is believed that many of the more bloodcurdling superstitions associated with the Mandrake – in particular its power to flee from prospective pickers on leg-like roots, or kill them off with its notorious shriek – were invented by professional Greek herb pickers, who were anxious to keep amateurs away from their livelihood. The same is probably true of many of the stories concerning the poisonousness of shellfish out of season, and all those confusing saws about Rs in the month. Shellfish are one of the lifelines by which coastal dwellers hang on to a measure of independence round the year. Yet they are also one of the most tempting of wild foods that are there just for the picking. Unhappily for the professionals, the next generation of pickings is being spawned just when the holidaymakers are trooping out to the mudflats with their buckets and spades. No wonder, then, that the gentle warnings of superstition, the one sort of 'Keep Out' notice permissible on public land, are propped up rather more than they would be by facts alone.

In fact every sort of fish is slightly out of condition during the breeding season, but none need be poisonous, not even shellfish. This is not to say that there are no good reasons for leaving shellfish alone during the summer months. Molluscs are highly susceptible to disease and temperature change, and unless the largest possible numbers are allowed to spawn freely, their survival rate will be low.

And ironically, the way we are currently treating our coastal waters may yet turn the story into sound advice. Bivalve molluscs (with shells in two hinged halves like castanets) feed by pumping water through their shells and filtering out the food particles. In doing this they may also filter out sewage particles and the enteric bacteria which are associated with them. During the warm weather which corresponds to the off-season these bacteria can multiply alarmingly, up to a level which can cause food poisoning in humans. Unfortunately this is particularly true of large bivalves like mussels and oysters, which filter a great deal of water each day, and sometimes seem to relish the warm, soupy conditions near sewage outlets.

So shellfish should be approached with caution, but not with trepidation, and with the knowledge that it is not some sinister springtime sap that makes them chancy during the warm months, but our own disgusting habits. If you keep to these few rules, you will never need a stomach pump:

1. Never gather them close to human dwellings, or anywhere where sewage or refuse is pumped into the sea.

2. Always wash them well, outside and in, in clean water.

3. Check that all your specimens are alive immediately before cooking them. Shellfish decompose very quickly after death, and a dead fish is more dangerous than a dirty one. To tell if a shellfish is alive, gently force its shell open a fraction of an inch. It should shut again quickly as soon as you take off the pressure. If it is already open, opens wide with ease, or fails to shut again, it is safer to assume that it is dead.

 Winkle *Littorina littorea* [A]

Widely distributed round all British coasts. Common on rocks and weeds on the middle shore. A sharply pointed shell, $\frac{1}{2}''$ to $1''$ high, spiralled like a tiny whelk, and normally dark grey in colour.

You will not need to spend very long unravelling a bowl of winkles from their tortuous shells before you appreciate why the process produced a new verb of extrication for the English language.

Judged purely as food, winkles do not have much to commend them. They have none of the rich flavour of mussels or the he-man texture of whelks. You need a dozen to provide a single mouthful. The joy of winkle eating lies wholly in the challenge of getting the things out of their shells, and, for the experienced, in the leisurely ritual of the pin and the twist. Dorothy Hartley describes a delightful encounter with a connoisseur:

'I learnt "winkles" from a night watchman. He used to sit by his big red coke fire-bucket, a bit of folded blanket over his knees, his mug of hot tea, and a little enamel bowl full of winkles. And he would turn up the little tab-end at the bottom of his waistcoat, pull out a long pin, and take a winkle. . . . And then he would chuck the empty shell neatly over his shoulder into the canal with a tiny "plop". He did it quite slowly, and he always paused (I can see him now, red in the fire-light, head aslant, his huge hand still half-open – curved like a hoary brown shell). He always paused just that second till he heard the tiny plop, before he bent and picked up the next winkle. His old woman had put him "a reet proper breakfast", and he had a basket with a bottle in it. But, as he said, "Winkles, they *do* pass the time along very pleasantly". From *Food in England*.

You can find winkles on almost every stretch of rocky or weedy shore between high and low tide-marks. They are often in quite large colonies, and can be easily gathered.

To clean the sand and grit out from them thoroughly, soak them in fresh water for about twelve hours. Whether this is overnight or not depends upon the state of your nerves. Winkles are determined creatures, and their efforts to return to the sea can sound positively eerie if you are not accustomed to them.

My own initiation into this disconcerting habit came from a bucketful left innocently in the sink of a friend's boat. At midnight the galley suddenly began to sound as if it was entering an advanced stage of disintegration. Soft cracks and splashes gathered in tempo, as if some high-speed dry rot was chewing through the woodwork.

Inside the galley, there were winkles everywhere: crawling over the floor, up the walls, dropping from the rim of the bucket like parachutists. It was a humbling display of determination and agility, and sentimental creatures that we were, we put the lot back in the sea.

You can keep the winkles in, and your conscience untroubled, by the simple device of a lid over your container. From then on the process is simple. When they have finished soaking, cook them by plunging them into boiling water and simmering for about ten minutes.

Then eat them like the night watchman, leisurely, with a long pin, and perhaps a little pepper and vinegar at the side. The whole fish is edible, except for the tiny mica-like plate at the mouth of the shell, which should be removed with your pin before you winkle out the flesh.

Cockle *Cardium edule* [A]

Widely distributed round all coasts. Common in sand or sandy mud on the middle shore. A rather dumpy, globular shell up to $2\frac{1}{2}''$ across. The two halves are heavily ribbed and are pale brown to grey-blue in colour.

Just after the tide has gone out over the vast saltmarshes on the north Norfolk coast, you will sometimes see a cluster of enormous slate coloured cockles strewn across the muddy sand like dice. These are the famous 'Stiffkey Blues', the best and fattest cockles of all. They are not dead, yet they seem stranded, curiously unconcerned about beginning their laborious burrow into the sand.

To find any cockles, big or small, as conspicuously displayed as this is a rare piece of luck. More often they are one to three inches under the surface. There is no simple rule about where they can be found between the tidelines. A vein of mud in the sand is a good sign; so is a green film of plankton over the surface. But the only sure test is to scratch about and see if they are there. Hands will do if you only want a few, but a rake with blunted points is the best way of pulling them out of the sand quickly. Gather them into a bucket or bag. Do not throw them; the shells break easily, and a broken cockle is very quickly a dead one. Don't pick any specimen less than one inch across either. It's scarcely worth the bother. And cockles, like all shellfish, wage a constant battle for survival against pollution and over-picking. If the young fish are taken before they have had a chance to spawn then the battle is bound to be a losing one. Many stretches of coast have experienced shellfish droughts recently, and though there is probably no single explanation, the over-picking of immature shells is certainly a contributing factor.

When you have all the cockles you want take them home and wash off the superficial mud and sand. Let them rinse themselves through in a bucket of clean fresh water for at least six hours, and preferably overnight. Then drop them into a saucepan of boiling water, checking each one for signs of life immediately before. They will quickly open, and be thoroughly cooked within five minutes.

The results can be made into soups or pies, or eaten plain as soon as they have been strained from the water. Try experimenting with sauces to go with the freshly cooked fish. A friend of mine once concocted one out of the improbable ingredients of yoghourt, mustard and horseradish, and it made a wonderfully tart, silky foil to the springy flesh of the cockles. One eighteenth century cookery book recommends that the cooked fish should be stuffed into slits in marsh lamb, as if the meat were larded with them.

My favourite way with cockles is to fry them with bacon. Cook the bacon very crisp first, then remove it from the pan and fry the cockles in its fat. Serve them together on toast with plenty of pepper.

Clam or Sand gaper *Mya arenaria* [A]

Widely distributed. Common in sand and sandy mud on the middle and lower shore. An oval shell not unlike a large mussel in shape, up to five inches across, coloured grey or brownish.

Sometimes when you are digging fairly deep for cockles you may come across some clams, large mussel-like shells with formidable protruding trunks. These are the siphons through which the fish feed whilst they are buried, and can be extended up to a foot in length.

Clams are big enough to need substantially more cooking than most shellfish. After the shells have been rinsed like cockles, they are scalded in boiling water for about ten minutes. The fish is then removed from the shell, the siphon usually trimmed off, and the remaining meat fried or baked for a further half an hour, or simply boiled until tender and served with a sauce.

Clam chowder, the American way with clams, is an elaborate dish, but consists basically of the simmering together of chopped clams, fried pieces of pork, onion and potato, with milk added as the soup comes off the boil.

(Beware of confusion over names, by the way. Large cockles are often called clams, as are scallops see p. 27.)

Limpet *Patella vulgata* [C]

Limpets are shaped like flat cones and cling to rocks. The

common limpet, *Patella vulgata*, is common enough on rocky shores, and can grow up to $2\frac{1}{2}''$ across. But it is normally somewhat smaller than this, and consequently a fair number – and a fair degree of scrambling – are needed to gather enough for a meal.

Do not pick them from piers or jetties, but from out-of-town rocks that are covered daily by the tide. They can be prised from the rocks with a knife or dislodged with a hefty kick. Soak them in the usual way and then boil like cockles until the meat floats free of the shell. Be warned, though: limpets can be very tough, and they may need considerable further simmering or baking. In the Isle of Man they fry them at Easter.

Mussels *Mytilus edulis* [C]

Mussels are amongst our commonest and most delectable shellfish. But they are also responsible for most cases of shellfish poisoning. This has been happening with such frequency recently that I felt that a C rating would have to be given to indicate the need for special caution.

It is not difficult to see why mussels are becoming increasingly infected. They pump at least ten gallons of water through their bodies every day. Given the condition of some of our coastal waters this is enough to enable a single fish to concentrate a substantial amount of contaminant over a period of months. There have also been plagues of a highly toxic plankton – the notorious 'red tides' – along many European coasts during recent breeding seasons. Mussels strain out these poisonous plants during their normal feeding, and concentrate the toxin in their livers to levels that can be dangerous for both birds and man. (Incidentally, the North American Indians, always wise and resourceful with wild foods, knew all about the dangers of these tiny plants. They would prohibit the taking of mussels until the 'red tide' had passed, and even set guards along the beaches.)

But if you follow the tips given on p. 22 you are very unlikely to eat a bad mussel. Gather them from clean stony shores at low tide outside the summer months, let them stand through at least two changes of fresh tap water and carefully check that each one is still alive before cooking.

As a change from moules marinières, try baking them in their shells in hot ash, and popping in a mixture of butter, garlic and parsley as the shells open.

Scallop or Clams *Pecten maximus* [C]

Scallops are the huge, classic shells that came to be the oil company's symbol. You find them occasionally on the lower shore – that strip of sand that is only uncovered during very low tides.

Like clams (p. 25) scallops need a substantial amount of cooking. After washing and scalding, cut away the white and orange fish, dust with flour or breadcrumbs and fry for about forty minutes. They have a superbly fleshy, almost poultry-like flavour.

Oyster *Ostrea edulis* [C]

Oysters have not always been the expensive delicacy that they are now. For centuries they were one of the great staples of working-class diet. In the fifteenth century 4d would buy eight gallons. As late as the mid-nineteenth, Dickens could make Sam Weller say:

'. . . poverty and oysters always seem to go together . . . the poorer a place is, the greater call there seems to be for oysters . . . here's a oyster stall to every half-dozen houses. The street's lined with 'em. Blessed if I don't think that ven a man's wery poor, he rushes out of his lodgings, and eats oysters in reg'lar desperation.'

But in the latter half of the nineteenth century prices suddenly rocketed, and there is little doubt that the cause was the irresponsible over-harvesting of the beds to meet the demands of expanding townships.

Today you will be lucky to find many wild oysters. The ones that still remain round our coasts are mostly under cultivation in private beds. So if you should chance upon one, clinging to a rock in some estuary or creek, best leave it where it is. But if eat it you must, there is only one way: raw, with lemon and paprika pepper.

Razor shell *Ensis siliqua* [C]

There is only one time and place when razor shells can be found alive in any numbers, and that is on clean sandy shores at the very edge of the lowest tides of the year. Even then they shoot into the sand at the slightest disturbance. The only way to retrieve them, short of frantic digging, is reputedly to pour salt into their escape holes, when they will rise ignominiously to the surface. Cook them like clams.

Nuts

The majority of plants covered by this book are in the 'fruit and veg' category. They make perfectly acceptable accompaniments or conclusions to a meal, but would leave you feeling a little peckish if you relied on nothing else. Nuts are an exception. They are the major source of second-class protein amongst wild plants. Walnuts, for instance, contain 18 per cent protein, 60 per cent fat, and can provide 3000 calories per pound of kernels.

It is therefore possible to substitute nuts for the more conventional protein constituents of a meal – as indeed vegetarians have been doing for centuries. But do not pick them to excess because of this. Wild nuts are crucial to the survival of many wild birds and animals, who have just as much right to them, and considerably more need.

Keep those you do pick very dry, for damp and mould can easily permeate nutshells and rot the kernel.

Hazel *Corylus avellana* [A]

Local names for nuts: COBNUT, FILBERT; FILBEARD, Glos, Oxf, Northants; HALE, HALSE, Corn, Dev, Som; HASKETTS, Dor; WOODNUT, Yorks.

Abundant throughout the British Isles, except in very damp areas. Grows in woods, hedgerows and scrubland. A shrub, 4 to 12 feet high, with roundish, downy, toothed leaves. Best known for the yellow male catkins, called 'lambs' tails', which appear in the winter. Nuts from late August to October, $\frac{1}{2}''$ to $1''$ long, ovoid and encased in a thick green lobed husk.

The problem with hazelnuts is that if you hold back from picking them until they are fully ripe, the squirrels and jays will get there first. If you pick whilst the nuts are still abundant on the trees in late August, they are soft and tasteless and apt to wither in their shells within a day. There is a curiosity about these times, for St Philibert's Day – from which the nut received one of its names in an attempt to exorcise its pagan associations – is on August 22. At this time some of the bigger green nuts will give you a crunchy mouthful if you eat them immediately, but they lack the dry, almost fishy flavour of the ripe brown cobs.

Late September is probably the best compromise. Searching for hazelnuts at this early autumn time is a pleasurable test of eye and reflexes. You must beat along the hedgerows like a hawk, trying to distinguish the nuts from the crinkly, parchment yellow of the changing leaves. If you see some, in bunches of two or three, go for them very carefully, for when they are ripe they will fall from the husks at the slightest vibration of the bush. If the ground cover under the bush is not as it usually is, an impenetrable tangle of nettle and dead leaves, but relatively clear ground or grass, then it is worthwhile giving the bush a shake. Even the invisible ripe ones should find their way on to the ground after this. In fact it is always worth searching the ground underneath a hazel. If there are nuts there which are dark or grey-brown in colour then the kernels will have turned to dust. But there is a chance that there will be some fresh windfalls that have not yet been picked on by the birds.

In spite of their apparent hardiness and ability to thrive in the British climate, hazels are not always successful at producing fruit. There are any number of pressures which can prevent the formation of nuts, as happened in 1969 when there were very few to be found. For a start, the bushes must be at least seven years old. They must be allowed to branch and produce catkins and flowers – which contemporary hedge-cutting techniques inhibits. The pollen from the catkins must succeed in reaching the delicate crimson stigmas of the female flowers, which appear in January. If the winds are too strong, or there are heavy frosts, both catkins and flowers can be destroyed.

Once you have gathered your nuts, keep them in a dry, warm place – but in their shells, so that the kernels don't dry out as well. You can use the nuts chopped or grated in salads, or with apple and raisins on raw oatmeal (muesli). Ground up in a blender, mixed with milk and chilled, they make a passable imitation of the Spanish drink *horchata*. But hazelnuts are such a rich food that it seems a little wasteful not to use them occasionally as a protein substitute. Weight for weight, in fact, they contain fifty per cent more protein, seven times more fat and five times more carbohydrate than hens' eggs. What better way of cashing in on such a meaty hoard than the unjustly infamous nut cutlet?

Melt two ozs of fat in a saucepan, and stir in the same weight of flour. Add a pint of stock and seasoning and stew for ten minutes, stirring all the time. Add three ozs of breadcrumbs and two ozs of grated hazelnuts. Cool the mixture and shape into cutlets. Dip the cutlets into an egg and milk mixture, coat with breadcrumbs and fry in deep fat until brown.

If you gather your nuts early, and have an interest in the more bizarre branches of cookery, you might like to pick some hazel leaves as well and try this fifteenth century recipe for a 'noteye'. It contains all the classic characteristics of the medieval style of cooking: extensive use of spices, the fine cutting and blending of all ingredients, and the gruel-like consistency of the final product.

'Take a great porcyoun of Haselle leuys, and grynd in a morter as small as you may whyl that they ben younge; take pan, and draw uppe a thrift of Mylke of Almaundys, y-blaunchyd and temper it with Freysshe brothe; wryng out clene the ius of the leuys; take Flysshe of Porke or of Capoun, and grynd it smal, and temper it uppe with the mylke, and caste it in a potte, and the ius there-to; do it ouer the fyre and late it boyle; take Flour of Rys, and a-lye it; take and caste sugar y-now ther-to and Vynegre a quantyte, and pounder Gyngere, and Safroun it wel, and Sall; take small notys, and breke hem; take the kyrnells, and make hem whyte and fye hem uppe in grece; plante there-with the meat and serve forth.'

Slightly adapted from *Two Fifteenth Century Cookbooks*

Sweet chestnut *Castanea sativa* [A]

Local names: SPANISH CHESTNUT, STOVER NUT, MEAT NUT, SARDIAN NUT, HUSKED NUT.

Well distributed throughout England, though scattered in Scotland. Fairly common in woods and parks. A tall, straight tree with single spear-shaped serrated leaves. Nuts in October and

November, two or three carried in spherical green cases covered with long spines.

A nut to get your teeth into. And a harvest to get your hands into, if the year is right and the nuts thick enough on the ground to warrant a small sack rather than a basket. Although the tree was in all probability introduced to this country by the Romans, nothing seems more nostalgically English than gathering and roasting chestnuts on fine autumn afternoons.

The best chestnut trees are the straight, old ones whose leaves turn brown early. (Don't confuse them, by the way, with horse chestnuts, whose inedible conkers look very similar to sweet chestnuts inside their spiny husks. In fact the trees are not related, *Castanea sativa* being a cousin of the oak.) They will be covered with the prickly fruit as early as September, and small specimens of the nuts to come will be blown down early in the next month. Ignore them, unless you can find some bright green ones which have just fallen. They are undeveloped and will shrivel within a day or two.

The ripe nuts begin to fall late in October, and can be helped on their way with a few judiciously thrown sticks. Opening the prickly husks can be a painful business, and for the early part of the crop it is as well to take a pair of gloves and some strong boots, the latter for splitting the husks underfoot, the former for extricating the fruits. (By mid-November this should be unnecessary, as most of the nuts will be lying free amongst the leaves.) The polished brown surface of the ripe nuts uncovered by the wound in the husk is positively alluring. You will want to stamp on every husk you see, and rummage down through the leaves and spines to see if the reward is glinting there.

Don't shy away from eating the nuts raw. If the stringy pith is peeled away as well as the shell, most of their bitterness will go. But roasting transforms them. They take on the sweetness and bulk of some tropical fruit. Like so much else in this book the excitement lies as much in the rituals of preparation as in the food itself. Chestnut roasting is an institution, rich with associations of smell, and of welcomingly hot coals in cold streets. To do it efficiently at home, slit the skins, and put the nuts in the hot ash of an open fire or close to the red coals – save one, which is put in uncut. When this explodes, the others are ready. The explosion is fairly ferocious, scattering hot shrapnel over the room, so sit well back from the fire and make sure all the other nuts *have* been slit.

Chestnuts are a highly versatile vegetable. They can be pickled, candied, or made into an amber with breadcrumbs and egg yolk. Boiled with brussel sprouts they were Goethe's favourite dish. Chopped, stewed and baked with red cabbage, they make a rich vegetable pudding.

Chestnut purée is probably the most adaptable form in which to use the nuts. Shell and peel the chestnuts, and boil them in a thin meat stock for about forty minutes. Strain off the liquid and then rub the nuts through a sieve, or mash them in a liquidiser. The resulting purée can be seasoned and used as a substitute for potatoes, or form the basis of stuffings and sweets.

Beech, *Fagus sylvatica* [A]

Widespread and common throughout the British Isles, especially on chalky soils. A stately tree, with smooth grey bark and leaves of a bright, translucent green. (See page 83 for what to do with these.) Nuts in September-October, four inside a prickly brown husk. When ripe this opens into four lobes, thus liberating the brown, three-sided nuts.

The botanical name *Fagus* originates from a Greek word meaning to eat, though in the case of the beech this is more likely to have referred to pigs than humans. This is not to say that beechmast – the usual term for the nuts – is disagreeable. Raw, or roasted and salted, it tastes not unlike young walnut. But the nuts are very small, and the collection and peeling of enough to make an acceptable meal is a tiresome business.

This is also an obstacle to the rather more interesting use of beechmast as a source of vegetable oil. Although I have never tried the extraction process myself, mainly because of a lack of suitable equipment, it has been widely used on the Continent, particularly in times of economic hardship. During the two World Wars in some areas of Germany, beechnuts were considered of such importance as a source of domestic oil that schoolchildren were given special holidays to gather them. The oil was extracted on a communal mill usually owned by one of the village's farmers.

I hope that some readers who have access to a small mill might also have a go.

Although beech trees only fruit once every three or four years, each tree produces a prodigious quantity of mast, and there is rarely any difficulty in finding enough. It should be gathered as early as possible, before the squirrels have pinched it, and before it has had a chance to dry out. The three-faced nuts should be cleaned of any remaining husks, dirt or leaves and then ground, shells and all, in a small oil-mill. (For those with patience, a mincing machine or a strong blender should work as well.) The resulting pulp should be put inside a fine muslin bag and put in a press or under a heavy weight to extract the oil.

For those able to get this far, the results should be worthwhile. Every pound of nuts yields as much as three fluid ozs of oil. The oil itself is rich in fats and proteins, and provided it is stored in well-sealed containers, will keep fresh considerably longer than many other vegetable fats.

Beechnut oil can be used for salads or for frying, like any other cooking oil. Its most exotic application is probably beechnut butter, which is still made in some rural districts in the USA, and for which there was a patent issued in this country during the reign of George I.

Oak, *Quercus robur* [C]

Acorns have been used as human food in times of famine, though like beechmast their chief economic use has been as animal fodder. The raw kernels are forbiddingly bitter to most palates, but chopped and roasted they can be used as a substitute for almonds.

The Californian Indians used acorns as one of the basic items in their domestic economy – a custom which some joyless anthropologist has christened balanophagy. The acorns were most often used in the form of a coarse-ground meal. But at some stage their bitterness had to be removed, and any number of ingenious techniques were employed towards this end. In the simplest the acorns were buried, with perhaps some ash or charcoal, and watered from time to time until they became sweet. The more complicated processes involved pulverising the nuts, and then leaching them inside a sand-filled basin with repeated doses of water. The result has been described by an American writer as

... a mush which has few characteristics normally associated by Americans with food: it tends (1) to have the consistency of a gelatinous, crunchy peanut butter, (2) to be gritty with sand, (3) to have a semifluorescent surface colour reminiscent of gentian violet, and (4) to have a flavour which is a cross between alumized sour cream and Grapenuts. All that really can be said in its favour is that it is an extremely substantial food, of which, with a little exposure, one can become extremely fond.

In Europe the most common recent use of acorns has been in the roast form, as a substitute for coffee. They were recommended for this role during the war. The kernels were chopped, roasted to a light brown colour, ground up, and then roasted again.

Walnut, *Juglans regia* [C]

The walnut was introduced to this country from Asia Minor four or five hundred years ago. It has rarely spread beyond those sites where it was planted and has consequently never been added to the British flora. Even these specimens have now been depleted because of the great popularity of walnut wood, particularly during the last century. But there are enough individual trees scattered around old woodland and parks to make the nut worth a mention here.

The Latin name *Juglans regia* can be very roughly translated as 'the nut of Jupiter', and very ambrosial the walnut is. Even in purely dietetic terms it makes an impressive showing, yielding over 3000 calories per pound, and in the green state three times as much Vitamin C as Ministry of Food orange juice. In France the nuts are so valued that land-owners assess the rental value of a mature walnut as the same as an acre of ploughland. Each tree can yield up to 150 lbs of nuts annually.

Walnuts are best when they are fairly ripe and dry, in late October and November. Before this, the young 'wet' walnuts are rather tasteless. If you wish to pick them young, pick them in

July whilst they are still green and make pickle from them. They should be soft enough to pass a knitting needle or skewer through. Prick them lightly with a fork to allow the pickle to permeate the skin, and leave them to stand in strong brine for about a week, until they are quite black. Drain and wash them and let them dry for two or three days more. Pack them into jars and cover them with hot pickling vinegar. Seal the jars and allow to stand for at least a month before eating.

Fungi

The thought of wild fungi raises a shudder in most people, including those who will cheerfully eat the contents of a vaguely labelled can of 'mushroom' soup. They are the most misunderstood and maligned of all wild foods. There are 3000 species of large-bodied fungi growing in the British Isles, yet only twenty-odd of these are seriously poisonous. Admittedly, four of these are fatally so, and many hundreds of the remainder inedible because of toughness, indigestibility or taste. But this scarcely seems sufficient to explain the blackening of the reputation of a whole biological category. Robert Graves has suggested that our hostility towards fungi may be a hangover from the time when there were religious taboos against their use by any persons outside the priesthood. I would think that there are more down to earth reasons than this. It would be foolish to pretend that the identification of fungi is as easy as the identification of flowering plants. They have fewer differentiating characteristics, and can vary enormously, inside one species, in shape, size and colour. Even though the number of poisonous species is, comparatively, very small, each one resembles maybe half a dozen edible types.

The *un*earthly qualities of fungi no doubt exaggerate these worries. They rise up quickly, in lightless places. Many of them thrive on the dead or dying remains of other plants – or worse, of animals. Their shapes can bear magical resemblances to other organisms, to corals, brains, ears, and unmentionable sexual parts.

But there is no doubt that much of the discomfort we feel about fungi is conditioned by culture and fashion. We do, after all, consume over 30,000 tons of cultivated mushrooms a year. So the idea of fungus, and the characteristically fungoid taste, are not in themselves repugnant. Attitudes can change, too. In Rome, the common mushroom itself was condemned in the middle of the last century. In France, where there are strong traditions of wild fungi use, over 30 species are sold commercially. But scarcity of food immediately after the last war led to the indiscriminate eating of many other species, and for a while only cultivated mushrooms were permitted to be sold in the large towns.

Today there is extensive use of wild fungi in many parts of the world. At the famous fungi market in Munich over 300 edible species are licensed to be sold. In Russia the authorities issue cheap permits for the national conifer forests, where enormous quantities of fungi (mainly *Lactarius deliciosus*) are gathered for drying for the winter.

There are over a hundred quite good edible species growing in this country and it is sad that so many of them go to waste. They have no especial food value (though they contain more protein than vegetables and considerable quantities of vitamin D) but some intriguing tastes and textures, and are worthwhile for this alone.

Readers who are familiar with other books on edible fungi may find my own selection rather curious. But to allay any possible worries I have chosen to describe only those species that have some combination of characteristics that makes them unmistakeable. Many common and excellent-tasting species, like the Fairy-ring champignon and the Honey fungus have consequently been relegated to an expert's list at the end of this section, since they are difficult to tell in the field.

There are no general rules about when and where the fungi I have included in this section can be found. They grow in all sorts of environments at all times of the year. But there are some guidelines which can be deduced from the way that fungi grow. Fungi are characterised as a class by the fact that they do not contain any chlorophyll, and are thus unable to manufacture their own carbohydrates. They must live off those manufactured by other plants, either living or dead. So any ground which is rich in root structure or newly decaying plant litter is potentially good as a fungus bed. Mature woodlands and well-established pasture are both ideal environments. The more these host environments flourish, die, regenerate, the better off will be their attendant fungi. So although fungi have no use for direct light, they do prosper in areas where the underground growth and cycling of their hosts is stimulated by light: hedges, woodland clearings and paths, etc. They also like warmth and damp, and a year which begins with a slow, fine summer, and continues with a wet, mild autumn, is likely to be as good for fungi as it is for other types of fruit. It is the right balance of sunlight, moisture and warmth which seems to be crucial. In wet summers fungi will tend to appear more in woodland clearings; in dry summers in the shady, moisture-retaining spots. Some fungi appear in the spring and others can live through the winter. But the greatest number appear in the late summer and disappear with the first hard frosts.

The following are a few suggestions about picking and preparation which apply to all fungi, and which will help guarantee you have good specimens this season, and more to come back to next.

Get a good field guide and learn the few poisonous species (Appendix 1) first. Only pick those which satisfy *all* the specifications about size, colour, time of year and environment that are given on the following pages. These have been chosen so that it is very difficult to make a mistake if you follow them to the letter.

Don't pick specimens which are so old that they have started to decay, or so young that they have not yet developed their identifying characteristics. Avoid gathering on very wet days; many fungi are highly porous, and a blewit, for instance, can soak up its own weight of water in a few hours. Moisture not only spoils the taste and texture but creates conditions where decomposition can proceed more quickly.

Don't cut fungi with a knife. You will need the whole stalk, and any sheath (or 'volva') for a full identification. Don't yank them out of the ground, either. The fungi we pick are simply the fruit bodies of the fungus plant proper, which is a complex net of fine threads called the mycelium growing around the roots, dead leaves, or whatever is the food source of the fungus. If this is broken by too careless picking, the plant can be damaged. The best way of picking a fungus is to twist it gently until it breaks free.

Gather your crop into an open, well-ventilated basket, not your pockets or a polythene bag. Fungi decay very quickly, and heat, congestion and stale air accelerate this process.

Go through all your specimens again carefully before cooking. Check their identification and discard any you are not confident about. Indigestion brought on by uncertainty about whether you have done yourself in can be just as uncomfortable as real food poisoning. Remember there are no infallible tricks with sixpences or salt which can identify all poisonous species.

To be especially careful cut each fungus in half and throw away any that are maggot-ridden or possessed of suspicious white gills (most of the deadly *Amanitas* have these). Also cut away decaying or wet pieces.

Clean the fungi before cooking. But there is no need to wash them or peel them, unless it is specifically stated in the text. Use them within 24 hours of picking.

In common with other new foods it is as well to try a fairly small portion the first time you eat any species. It is just possible that it may 'disagree with you'.

Having prepared your fungi there are many other ways of using them than the recipes given here for each individual species. Drying is a useful way of preserving them for the winter. To dry fungi, cut prepared specimens into slices about 1/8" thick, and keep in a warm place or a dry current of air. Threading the slices (or the whole caps of smaller specimens) on to a string is a convenient and attractive way of doing this. They are dry when they feel crisp to the fingers and can be easily crumbled into small pieces. The fungi can be reconstituted by boiling in water for about twenty minutes.

Fungi can also be pickled by simmering in water for about ten minutes, draining and being put in jars under ordinary pickling vinegar.

There is also enormous scope for a whole new range of fungi recipes based on a view of them as fruits, not savouries. Experiment with fungi in cakes and puddings, and stewed with sugar like plums.

Sparassis *Sparassis crispa* [A]

Not uncommon at the base of pine stumps or trees, August to November. Resembles a large round sponge, or the heart of a cauliflower. The colour varies with age, from pale cream to ochre. Size: about a foot across with *flat*, twisted and very divided branches.

The only slightly dangerous species with which *Sparassis*

could conceivably be confused is *Ramaria formosa*, which is rare, and has pink, *rounded* branches.

If you are lucky enough to find a *Sparassis* nestling at the bottom of a pine (the Swiss call it 'the Broody Hen') it should be cut off from its thick fleshy stalk with a knife. Only young specimens should be gathered as the old ones are tough and bitter.

Cut the *Sparassis* into sections and remove any brown or spongy parts. Then wash thoroughly to remove any dirt and insects from the folds. An old recipe for very young specimens is to bake them in a casserole with butter, parsley, a little garlic, and some stock and seasoning. They taste mild and pleasantly nutty.

Rather older specimens are best dried until they are brittle, for future use as flavouring.

Chanterelle *Cantharellus cibarius* [A]   Pl. 1

Fairly common in all kinds of woodland, but especially beech, between July and December. Shaped like a funnel, one to three inches across. Egg-yolk yellow in colour and smelling slightly of apricots. Gills like fan-vaulting or veins, shallow, much forked and continuous with the stem. No ring.

'You find them, suddenly, in the autumn woods, sometimes clustered so close that they look like a torn golden shawl dropped amongst the dead leaves and sticks.'

So Dorothy Hartley described this most exquisite of fungi. An eighteenth century writer said that if they were placed in the dry mouths of dead men they would come to life again.

Because they are seldom attacked by insects, and cannot be confused with any dangerous species, chanterelles ('girolles') are perhaps the most used of all wild fungi on the Continent. They are slightly tougher than some other fungi and should be stewed slowly in milk for at least ten minutes. The result is delicately perfumed and slightly peppery.

Perhaps because of colour sympathy chanterelles have always been associated with eggs, and there is scarcely any better way of serving previously cooked specimens than in omelettes or with scrambled eggs.

Two fairly common close relations of the chanterelle can be treated in much the same way.

Horn of plenty *Craterellus cornucopoides* [B]

Fairly common in leafy woods, especially beech, August to November. Funnel-shaped, with a heavy, crinkled margin to the cap, up to five inches high, browny black in colour. Lower surface of cap continuous with stem, and smooth or slightly wrinkled. No ring.

Good for drying.

Cantharellus infundibuliformis [B]

Fairly common in clusters in all kinds of woodland, July to January. Funnel-shaped, with a slightly crinkled margin. Cap: an inch or two across and dark brown. Stem deep yellow. Gills, fold-like and branched as in the chanterelle. No ring.

Wood hedgehog *Hydnum repandum* [A]　　　　　　　　Pl. 1

Common in all kinds of woodland, August to November. The cap is irregularly shaped, about 2″ to 4″ across and is covered with a buffish to pink skin, smooth and often cracked, like fine leather. The 'gills' take the form of unmistakeable tiny white spines, of unequal length. Stem: short, stout, whitish. No ring.

The genus *Hydnum* is unique amongst fungi in having spines instead of gills, and all the commoner species having this characteristic are edible.

The wood hedgehog is the commonest species and is good to eat once its slightly bitter taste has been removed. This is best done by boiling the chopped fungus for a few minutes and then draining off and discarding the water. Then boil in milk or stock for a further twenty minutes. Serve on toast with a dash of sherry sprinkled over the top.

Blewits *Tricholoma saevum* [A]　　　　　　　　Pl. 1

Not uncommon in grassy pastures, October to December. The cap is flattish with an incurving marginal edge, two to five inches across, dry to touch but slightly jellyish and translucent, pale brown to greyish in colour. Gills: crowded, white to greyish-pink. Stem: stout, tinged with blue and occasionally swollen at the base. No ring. Flesh white and firm.

Blewits (named after the bluish-violet tinge of their stems) were one of the few fungi sold commercially in Britain. The trade was especially strong in the Midlands, and it is from there that the traditional way of cooking blewits as tripe comes.

Blewits often grow in large rings, and it is easy to overlook them in the late autumn, for their flat irregular caps look like dead leaves scattered over the field. Pick them on a dry day (they are very porous), clean, and chop off their stems. Then cut up the stems finely with an equal amount of onions and pack round the caps with a little chopped sage and bacon fat. Just cover the blewits with milk and simmer for half an hour. Pour off the liquid, thicken with flour and butter and seasoning and pour back over the fungi mixture. Simmer for another quarter of an hour, and then serve the whole mixture inside a ring of mashed potatoes, with toast and apple sauce.

This way of cooking the fungi is probably not entirely fortuitous, for their aromatic taste and jellyish texture are indeed reminiscent of tripe, though they are considerably more digestible.

Wood blewits *Tricholoma nudum* [B]

Fairly common in mixed woodlands and gardens, September to December. Much like the blewit, but bluish or violet all over when young. Cap: two to four inches across, turning reddish with age. Gills crowded, stem stout and mealy and always a little swollen at the base. No ring. Flesh tinged with violet at first, becoming whiter with age. Sweet smelling.

Oyster mushroom *Pleurotus ostreatus* [A]   **Pl. 1**

Common round the year, though principally in autumn, on dead or dying branches of beech and ash. This is a bracket fungus, growing off the branch or trunk in shelves up to six inches across. The cap is shell-shaped, convex at first, then flat, black to slate in colour. Gills white and deep. Flesh: white, soft, rubbery.

The oyster mushroom tends to be rather tough, and consequently requires long and careful cooking. But when you find it, it is usually possible to gather considerable quantities from the clusters in which it invariably grows, so it should not be passed over. Try slicing into pieces not more than half an inch thick, sprinkling with a few drops of lemon juice, turning in seasoned flour, then beaten egg and finally breadcrumbs. The slices should then be fried in deep oil until golden.

The fungus also dries well.

Flammulina velutipes [A]   **Pl. 1**

Common in clusters on stumps and trunks between September and March. The caps are thin, about one to three inches across, sticky and glistening, and honey yellow to orange red in colour. Gills broad and pale yellow. Stem thin, tough, often curved. Dark brown in colour and covered with a dark velvety down. The flesh is thin, whitish and rubbery with no smell.

This is one of the few fungi able to survive through frosts. During the winter months there is consequently very little chance that it might be confused with any other species. Use in stews or dry.

Parasol mushroom *Lepiota procera* [A]   **Pl. 1**

Quite common in wood margins, grassy clearings, roadsides, July to November. A large fungus, up to seven inches across. When young the cap resembles an old fashioned, domed beehive. It then spreads out flat but always retains its central prominence. It is dry, scaly, brown to grey-brown. Gills: white and detached from the stem. Stem: tall, slender, hollow and bulbous at the base and slightly scaly like the cap. Large white double ring which eventually becomes completely free of the stem so that it can be moved up and down.

The parasol is one of the best of our edible fungi. It is also one of the most distinctive, and can be seen from afar because of its size and preference for open spaces. The parasol rises closed, held to the stem by its large white ring. It then breaks free and opens like an umbrella. For the best combination of size and tenderness it should be picked just when the cap begins to open.

To cook, remove the stems and fry the caps quickly in oil or butter like common mushrooms. Because of their shape young parasols are also ideal for stuffing. Choose specimens that are still cup-shaped, cut off and discard the stems and fill with a sage and onion stuffing (or with mince or sausage meat if you want a more substantial dish). Arrange them their natural way up in a baking dish and fasten a small strip of bacon fat to the top of each parasol with a skewer. Cook in the oven for about half an hour, basting once or twice.

Shaggy parasol *Lepiota rhacodes*　[B]

Not uncommon on rich ground, though prefers more shade than the common parasol. July to November. Very similar to previous species, but cap is scalier and stem quite smooth. Flesh white but reddens on cutting.

Field mushroom *Agaricus campestris*　[A]　　　　**Pl. 1**

Locally common in pastures and meadows, August to November. Cap white, one to three inches across. Gills pink at first, darkening to brown. Stem short with a ring which in young specimens is joined to the cap. No sheath at base of stem, and no unpleasant smell.

Mushrooms have a special liking for meadows manured by horses, and the passing of horse-drawn transport has seriously affected the abundance of mushroom fields. There was a time when such fields might experience a 'white-out', when the precisely right combination of temperature, humidity and soil condition produced so many mushrooms simultaneously that the field appeared to have been covered overnight by snow. I have heard of this happening to lucky villages and of every portable container up to the size of the local bus being commandeered to take the crop in.

But if this is an almost unheard-of occurrence now, the field mushroom is very far from extinct. There are few grazing meadows which fail to produce some during the autumn months, even in the most improbable settings:

On Friday at 5.15 p.m. I gathered two pounds of fine mushrooms in Berkeley Square, London W1, just inside the gate at the Landsdown end to be exact, a couple of yards from the traffic and evidently ignored or mistrusted by the many passers-by. May I express my appreciation to Westminster Council for the welcome free garnish to this morning's breakfast, tonight's casserole and the weekend's coq au vin.

(Letter in Evening Standard, Oct 5, 1970)

Mushrooms are, paradoxically, one of the less easy fungi to identify exactly. There is virtually nothing which could be mistaken for a sparassis or a chanterelle, but one or two white-capped meadow fungi which can be taken for mushrooms by the careless. But if you study cultivated mushrooms carefully, and go only for pink-gilled, sheathless specimens from the wild, you are very unlikely to make a mistake.

Gathering mushrooms is a skill which has to be learned. They do not loom up above the grass like fairy story illustrations. In the rather dense pasture that is their natural habitat they are sometimes only visible as bright white patches in the grass when you are almost on top of them. You must train your eyes to scan no more than a few feet in front of you as you methodically quarter a field. When you find one, examine the area around it especially thoroughly, as mushrooms, like other fungi, tend to grow in colonies from the parent mycelium.

When you have your mushrooms check them again to make sure there are none with greenish tinged or warty caps, or with remnants of sheath at the bottom of the stems. And until you are expert at recognising the 'jizz' of mushrooms it is as well to be doubly cautious and cut each specimen in half vertically. Discard any with pure white gills, or that quickly stain pink or yellow. The Blusher (*Amanita rubescens*) and the Yellow-staining mushroom (*Agaricus xanthodermus*) can both be mistaken for the field mushroom, and though neither of them is dangerously poisonous, they can cause alarming digestive disturbances.

There is no need to peel mushrooms – indeed the taste will be diminished if you do. Simply wipe the caps with a dampish cloth and cut off the base of the stem. The very best way of cooking mushrooms is to fry them in bacon fat as soon as possible after collecting. The secret is to give them no more than three or four minutes in the pan. Field mushrooms tend to contain more water than cultivated, and if they are cooked for too long, they stew in their own liquid and become limp and mushy. Making soup from your wild mushrooms avoids this danger. Simply simmer the chopped caps and stems in seasoned milk for about half an hour with no other ingredients at all. The result is a delightfully smooth, light soup which is good hot or cold.

Young mushrooms can be used raw in salads, and the old ripe black ones for making ketchup (see Shaggy cap for recipe).

Horse mushroom *Agaricus arvensis* [A]

Very like a large field mushroom. Grows in similar habitats and at the same time of year. Can be up to one foot across when mature. Gills more greyish than in the field mushroom, smells pleasantly of almonds. Otherwise identification characteristics identical.

This close cousin of the field mushroom is also becoming uncommon. But it is a large, meaty and flavourful fungus, and if you only succeed in finding one mature specimen you have enough for a hefty meal.

It would be criminal to hack these big mushrooms up, so test for the Blusher and the Yellow-stainer, if you are unsure, by cutting off a thin strip near the edge.

If they are still dome-shaped they can be stuffed with whole tomatoes; if they are flat, grilled whole like steaks. An unusual recipe for either type is to stew them in milk, drain, set in a dish of white sauce, and then garnish with whole redcurrants made hot to the point of bursting. The dish is a contrast in colour and texture: the bright and sharp against the dark and fleshy.

Shaggy cap *Coprinus comatus* [A]

Local Names: INK CAP, INKYTOP, INKHORN, LAWYER'S WIG.

Common in fields, road verges, playing fields, rubbish tips, June to November. Cap almost cylindrical at first, 2″ to 5″ high, white

47

and covered with shaggy woolly scales. Opens to resemble a limp umbrella. Gills white at first, then pink to black as the cap opens, finally dissolving into an inky fluid. Stem: white and smooth with a small white ring at first.

The shaggy cap has a happy preference for grassland that is grazed by humans rather than animals. It can often be found in large numbers in the short mown grass by roadsides, and even in the thin stripes between dual carriageways. It comes up like a white busby and can scarcely be mistaken for any other species, save perhaps its close relative *Coprinus atramentarius*. This too is edible, but produces a curious reaction if eaten together with alcohol. It has been found to contain a chemical identical with the active ingredient of Antabuse, a drug which is used in the treatment of chronic alcoholism. When taken with alcohol it produces nausea and vomiting. *Coprinus atramentarius* can be distinguished by its dirty grey colour, its absence of scales, its generally more slender build and lack of ring.

The shaggy cap should be gathered whilst the cap is still closed and the gills still white. It should be cooked as soon as possible after picking, before the cap starts to dissolve. Take off the stems and bake in a very slow casserole with cream for up to two hours. The taste is pleasant and mild, but perhaps a little too innocuous to some palates.

The best way with shaggy caps may be to capitalise on their deliquescent nature and turn them into ketchup. Put the young caps into an earthenware jar, pack them down well and strew each layer with salt. When the jar is full put it in the oven, and simmer for an hour or two, being careful not to lose too much liquid by evaporation. Then strain through muslin, and for each quart of liquid add an ounce of black pepper and a scrape of nutmeg. Boil up again, strain into clean (preferably sterilised bottles) and seal well. The ketchup will keep indefinitely, but should be used quickly once opened.

Pholiota mutabilis [A]

Common in clusters on tree stumps from April onwards. Cap: dark brown and slightly sticky when damp, drying from the centre to a pale chamois-leather colour. 1″ to 3″ across. Gills cinnamon. Stem: dark brown and scaly up to the prominent ring; above ring, pale brown and smooth.

One of the earliest fungi to appear, and difficult to confuse with any other species if it is picked in the spring.

Although the caps are rather small and thin-fleshed, the clusters can contain literally hundreds, and certainly enough for a good meal. The fungus has an agreeable flavour, and is excellent for flavouring soups and stews, to which it gives a rich brown colour.

Cep *Boletus edulis* [A]   Pl. 1

Quite common in rides and clearings in all sorts of woods, especially beech, August to November. Cap, brown, dry and smooth, 2″ to 6″ across. Gills in *Boletus* are replaced by pores, much like sponge rubber in appearance, and in *Boletus edulis*, yellow to olive-brown in colour. Stem short and bulging, pale brown streaked with white. No ring. Flesh white and firm, and pleasant smelling.

All the members of the *Boletus* family are happily distinguishable by their 'gills', which are a spongy mass of fine tubes leading from the cap. The cep has the additional distinction of looking exactly like a glossy penny bun, to which it is always compared.

Ceps are one of the most famous of all edible fungi and at one time there were six different varieties for sale at Covent Garden. Unfortunately they are equally well liked by insects, so it is as well to cut the caps in half before cooking to check that they are not infested. To prepare for cooking remove the stem, and scoop away the pores with a spoon (unless they are very young and firm).

There are a prodigious number of recipes for ceps. They can be sliced and fried in oil for ten minutes with a little garlic and parsley. They can be fried with potatoes, or grilled with fish. They are excellent for drying, (and indeed, in the dried form are quite widely available in delicatessens in this country).

One of the most attractive is an old Polish recipe for beetroot and cep soup, which is served on Christmas Eve.

Make some clear beetroot stock by boiling chopped raw beet-roots in water, with bay leaves and peppercorns.

Take your sliced ceps and fry in butter with chopped onion and paprika pepper for about five minutes.

Take some ravioli-shaped pasta cases and fill with the cep and onion mixture, minced fine. Seal the cases, and bake in the oven until golden-brown.

Reheat the beetroot stock, and sharpen to taste with a little vinegar and lemon juice. At the last minute add the hot cases and serve.

Most Boletus species are mild and nutty to taste.

There are a large number of different species of *Boletus* growing in the British Isles, and all of them have the same foam-like gill structure. None of them is seriously poisonous if well-cooked, but a few are indigestible or can cause bad gastric upsets. Luckily all of these are tinged red or purple on pores or stem, and so are easily avoidable. None of the edible species listed below has this feature.

Boletus cyanescens [B]

Rare in woods on poor soil, especially spruce, August to November. Cap 2″ to 3″ across, rough, pale ochre in colour. Pores white to pale yellow. Stem stout, velvety and pale ochre in colour. The flesh is white but turns deep blue immediately after cutting.

Boletus luteus [B]

Quite common amongst grass in conifer woods, September to November. Cap 2″ to 3″ across, orange-brown, tinged with purple, and slimy to the touch. Pores white to pale yellow. Stem yellow, with a brownish-purple ring. Flesh yellow, unchanging when cut.

(Peel before cooking. Will not keep and therefore unsuitable for drying.)

Boletus elegans [B]

Quite common in larch woods only, March to November. Cap 2″ to 4″ slimy, pale yellow. Pores sulphur yellow. Stem tall, yellowish brown, with a distinctive yellow ring. Flesh has the colour and texture of rhubarb and stains pale lilac on cutting.

Boletus badius [B]

Quite common under conifers, August to November. Very similar to *Boletus edulis*. Cap 2″ to 4″ across, chestnut to chocolate brown, felt-like when dry, but slightly clammy when wet. Pores pale-yellow to yellow-green. Stem yellow-brown, stout and often curved, and striated. Flesh white to pale yellow, stains pale blue when cut.

Boletus subtomentosus [B]

Quite common in all sorts of wood, especially in moss and on grassy paths, June to October. Cap 2″ to 3″ across, colour varied, olive-yellow to brown; when old the surface is often cracked. Pores bright yellow. Stem yellow-brown, ribbed, tapering towards the base. Flesh soft, yellowish-white, pleasant smelling.

Boletus granulatus [B]

Quite common in conifer woods, June to October. Cap 2″ to 3″ across, slimy, straw-yellow to leather-brown. Peels easily. Pores yellow to olive, and when young exudes milky drops. Stem slender, light yellow. Flesh yellowish, unchanging when cut, fruity to smell. (Very susceptible to maggots.)

Boletus scaber [B]

Common in grass under birches, July to November. Cap 2″ to 4″ across, smooth and greyish-brown, dry, but sticky in wet weather. Gills white to dirty fawn. Stem tall, white, flecked with brown to black scales. Flesh soft, white, soon becoming moist and spongy. (Usually fairly free of maggots.)

Boletus testaceoscaber [B]

Common under birches and conifers, July to November. Cap 3″ to 7″ across, orange-yellow to yellow brown. Pores minute, dirty grey. Stem sturdy and tapering towards the cap, slate coloured, scurfy. Flesh white, very slowly turning dirty pink on cutting. (Don't be alarmed by the fact the flesh turns black on cooking.)

Giant puffball *Lycoperdon giganteum* [A]   **Pl. 1**

Not uncommon in woods, fields and under hedges. August to October. A large spherical fungus, 4″ to 12″ across, white, smooth and leathery initially, turning yellow to green when old. Grows apparently straight from the ground, with little or no stalk. Flesh solid, spongy, and pure white when young.

I think that if I had to choose my own favourite species from this book it would be the giant puffball. To come upon one of these suddenly is an astonishing experience, only rivalled by the taste of the first mouthful. There is not much point in searching deliberately for them; they are always unexpected, glinting like huge displaced eggs under a hedge or in the dark corner of a copse. If you are anything like me you will quickly strike up a strong affection for your ball, and cradle it back to be weighed and measured. It always seems sad to butcher the soft, kid-leather skin; but when you do, and cut through the flesh, the great flaky slabs of white meat that fall away are just as inviting.

Giant puffballs can grow to a prodigious size. Some have been found four feet in diameter, and the record specimen, discovered in New York State in 1877, was mistaken for a sheep at a distance. The usual size is more like a small football, but even this will provide a feast for a large number of people, for every part of the fungus is solid, edible flesh.

The only important quality to look out for is that this flesh is still pure white. As they age puffballs turn yellowish brown, and finally dissolve into a dust which consists of the reproductive spores. The giant puffball is one of the most fecund of all living organisms, and a single specimen may produce up to seven billion spores. If all of these germinated successfully and produced similar specimens with equally successful spores, their grand-children would form a mass eight hundred times the volume of the earth.

There is no real need to peel your puffball, though the skin may be too leathery for some tastes. One simple but excellent way to cook it is to slice it into large steaks about half an inch thick. Fry these, straight or battered, in bacon fat for about ten minutes until they are golden brown. The slices taken from the smoother, more rubbery flesh near the top of the fungus are like sweetbreads; the more crumbly steaks from near the base are as succulent as toasted marshmallow.

A more reverent way of dealing with such an elegantly shaped fungus – though I have never tried it myself – would be to bake it whole in the oven. The puffball would need to be well hollowed-out, and stuffed with a mixture of the chopped hollowings, some minced fat meat, preferably bacon, and some parsley and season-ing. The whole to be wrapped in foil and cooked fairly slowly in a low oven.

There are a number of different species of puffball growing in this country, all resembling, more or less, miniature versions of the giant puffball. All are edible when young and white-fleshed. But there is a species of a related family, the common earth-ball, which can cause gastric upsets if eaten in quantity. This resembles a puffball in shape, but its surface is hard, brown and scaly. So it is as well to pick only those puffballs which are white or creamy, and relatively smooth skinned.

It is usual to peel these smaller balls, as the skin can be tougher than the giant puffball's. This, together with the cutting of the base, will tell you if the flesh is white inside. These smaller balls can be cooked like *Lycoperdon giganteum*, or stewed whole in milk.

The commonest species is the common puffball:

Common puffball *Lycoperdon perlatum*   [B]

Very common in pastures, heaths and sometimes woods, from June to November. 1″ to 3″ across. More pear shaped than spherical, skin white to cream when young, usually covered with tiny, spiny pimples.

Jew's ear *Auricularia auricula* [A]

Quite common on elder trees throughout the year, especially October and November. An ear-shaped bracket fungus, 1″ to 3″ across, usually growing in clusters. Red-brown in colour, and gelatinous and soft when young. Upper surface more velvety and brown, underside more pink.

I can imagine no food more forbidding in appearance than the Jew's ear. It hangs in folds from decaying elder branches like slices off some ageing kidney, clammy and jelly-like to the touch. It is no fungus to leave around the house if you have sensitive relations, or even to forget about in your own pocket.

But it is a good edible species for all that, and is much prized in China, where a related species is grown for food on oak palings. It was also valued by the old herbalists (as 'fungus sambuci') as a poultice for inflamed eyes, though apparently not sufficiently to warrant a more complimentary name; 'Jew's meat' was the deprecatory term for all fungi in the Middle Ages. (Though the name may contain an oblique reference to Judas, who reputedly hanged himself from an elder tree.)

Jew's ear should be gathered whilst it is still soft (it turns rock-hard with age) and cut from the tree with a knife. It should be washed well, and sliced finely, for although the translucent flesh is thin, it can be tough and indigestible. Stew for a good three-quarters of an hour in stock or milk, and serve with plenty of pepper. The result is crisp and not unlike a seaweed.

Morel *Morchella esculenta* [C]

A fungus of great reputation and long standing, though now sadly rare. It grows in the spring in wood clearings, hedges and gardens, especially on chalky soils. It also has a curious liking for burnt places, and there were many records of colonies springing up on bomb sites in the war. In Germany in the eighteenth century, the peasant women even went to the length of starting forest fires to encourage growth!

The morel is a distinctive fungus, having a cap which resembles a cross-section of a honeycomb. It consequently needs to be washed well to remove any dirt or insects from the pits. It is usually blanched in boiling water before cooking. Morels make a good addition to stews and soups and being hollow they are also good stuffed and baked. But they are most commonly used for drying.

Truffle *Tuber aestivum* [C]   **Pl.** 1

Truffles are all but impossible to find without specially trained animals. But there was once a lively traffic in them in some of the southern counties of England, where they were sniffed out of beech woods by Spanish poodles. It was a fascinating business, as this account shows, and worth reviving, for there is no reason why the truffles themselves should be any less plentiful.

'With the retirement in 1930 of Alfred Collins, the last of the professional truffle hunters, the English truffle industry ceased to exist, having been carried out in the Winterslow area of Wiltshire traditionally for 300 years. Truffles are a kind of underground fungus or mushroom, mostly about the size of a golf ball, blue-black in colour when fresh, turning to brown-black. The outside has a somewhat warty appearance and inside the flesh is yellow-white with an average weight of a few ounces. In themselves there is not a great amount of taste but they have the virtue of spicing and bringing out the flavour of the ingredient they are cooked with, making them a highly-prized delicacy.

In England they were found almost exclusively around the roots of beeches growing about three inches underground. The season lasted from November till March and Alfred Collins hunted for them far and wide with two trained dogs. . . . If hunting within about 20 miles of his home, Alfred Collins cycled, carrying one dog in a special leather bag while the other ran, changing them over every five miles. Both were carried home, however, after a tiring day's work. . . . The dogs have to be carefully looked after to avoid spoiling their noses; young ones are trained by tying them to an older one with a coupling strap. In its early days, the dog had a truffle rubbed on its nose to give it the scent. The dogs would dig up the truffles, usually being helped in the digging with a special small pronged fork so they would not become tired with their long exertions. On finding a truffle, the dog would pick it up in its mouth and the hunter had to remove it fairly quickly or the dog would eat it. Dogs were rewarded with pieces of bread.

Pigs do not seem to have been much used in this country, which seems a little strange, as they hunt for truffles naturally, whereas dogs have to be trained. Normally, the hunter worked up wind and his dogs could scent the truffles frequently from a distance of 20 yards upwards. Truffles were invariably sold to private customers so they rarely came on the market. They only kept for about four days before losing flavour so they were always posted off as soon as possible in cardboard shoe boxes, which the children collected from the bootmaker for a penny each. Any not despatched were eaten by children on bread and butter. They could be preserved in vinegar. Like mushrooms they grew and then dispersed fairly quickly, the process taking about two days. If they grew more than 6″ below the ground they were not much good.

Alfred Collins could smell truffles and feel them underfoot and sometimes located them by the presence of a small cloud of flies in their vicinity. Some days, he drew completely blank, but on his best days he collected as many as 25 lbs. In about 1920, he put the price up to 2s 6d per pound, and by the time he retired he was able to get 5s 6d per pound. Even so, he died a poor man. His father once found a truffle weighing over 2 lb, which he sent to Queen Victoria, who replied saying she would send him her portrait. In due course, a sovereign arrived with her effigy on it.'

Condensed from 'Truffle Hunting in England'
by J. E. Manners, *Country Life*, 7 Jan, 1971

Fairy club *Clavaria pistillaris* [C]

An uncommon fungus looking exactly like a tiny yellow Indian club, or pestle. It grows to about 2″ or 3″ on woodland floors between September and December, and should be cooked like a common puffball.

Hericium coralloides [C]

A rare and very striking fungus which grows from the dead trunks of trees, especially beech. It has a thick central trunk and branches from which hang bunches of yellow tassles. It is good if picked young, washed and stewed well.

Sarcodon imbricatum   [C]

A close relative of the wood hedgehog (see p. 42). It is a con-ventionally shaped cap fungus, greyish brown in colour, with a scaly cap and the usual spiny gill structure of the *Hydnum* family. It occurs occasionally in sandy conifer woods between August and November, particularly in hilly districts. It has an excellently strong, spicy flavour, and is consequently useful as a flavouring.

Beefsteak fungus *Fistulina hepatica*   [C]

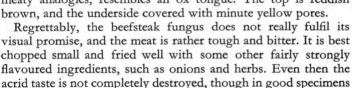

This is an aptly named bracket fungus, for the flesh when cut looks and feels like prime raw beef. It occurs occasionally on living trees, especially oak, and on the outside, to continue with meaty analogies, resembles an ox tongue. The top is reddish brown, and the underside covered with minute yellow pores.

Regrettably, the beefsteak fungus does not really fulfil its visual promise, and the meat is rather tough and bitter. It is best chopped small and fried well with some other fairly strongly flavoured ingredients, such as onions and herbs. Even then the acrid taste is not completely destroyed, though in good specimens it is not unpleasantly reminiscent of unripe tomatoes.

Anise cap *Clitocybe odora*   [C]

A small fungus which occurs in the litter of mixed woodlands in late summer and autumn. The whole fungus is a uniform blue-green colour, and has a strong, unmistakeable smell of aniseed. This persists on drying, and either fresh or dried the anise cap is used as a flavouring.

Russula vesca   [C]

I thought for some time about where to put the *Russulas* in this section. They are a difficult family, multi-specied, enormously variable in colouring and yet too good to omit altogether. Their variability can lead almost any specimen, at some stage in its development, to become one of those vague white-gilled, yellowish, greenish, or brownish capped fungi which are so difficult to tell from the main poisonous species. Hence the C grading, in spite of the fact that none of the *Russulas* themselves are poisonous when cooked. *Russula vesca* is probably the easiest of the common species to identify. It grows in all sorts of woods, especially oak and beech, from June to November. The cap is 2″ to 4″ across, and can be coloured anything from pale pink to violet or rusty red. Stem and gills are pure white, and there is no ring or sheath. The best identifying feature is that when the fungus is mature one or two millimetres of the margin of the cap are free from skin, and finely grooved with radial veins.

Cooked like *Boletus*, they are an excellent fungus, firmer than most, and with a mildly nutty taste which has been likened to new potatoes.

Other species of edible *Russula* are included in the list on p. 59.

The following is a list of those additional species of fungi that are regarded as edible. Some have been relegated to this section because they are indifferent as food, some because they are rare, most because of the difficulty of identifying them in the field. This is really a list for experts only: do not try anything on it unless you are well acquainted with the species, and absolutely confident in your identification.

Agaricus langei
Agaricus silvaticus
Agaricus augustus
Agaricus bisporus
Agaricus bitorquis
Agaricus subperonatus
Agaricus silvicola, Wood mushroom
Agaricus arvensis
Amanita vaginata, Grisette
Amanita fulva, Tawny Grisette
Amanita rubescens, The Blusher
Armillaria mellea, Honey Fungus
Boletus pulverulentus
Boletus erythropus
Cantharellus cinereus
Clavaria fistulosa
Clitocybe nebularis

Clitocybe flaccida
Clitocybe geotropa
Clitocybe gigantea
Clitocybe cyathiformis
Clitopilus prunulus
Coprinus atramentarius
Cortinarius albo-violaceus
Cortinarius varius
Hygrophorus niveus
Hygrophorus pratensis
Hygrophorus camarophyllus
Hygrophorus puniceus
Hygrophoropsis aurantiaca
Lactarius volemus
Lactarius deliosus
Lepiota excoriata
Lepiota leucothites
Limacella guttata

Laccaria amethystina
Lycoperdon caelatum
Lyophyllum decastes
Lyophyllum connatum
Marasmius oreades, Fairy-ring
   Champignon
Melanogaster variegatus
Morchella vulgaris
Morchella conica
Morchella semi-libera
Pluteus cervinus
Pluteus atromarginatus
Psathyrella lacrymabunda
Phaeolepiota aurea
Ramaria boytris
Ramaria flava
Russula claroflava
Russula cyanoxantha

Russula violeipes
Russula virescens
Russula xerampelina
Russula atropurpurea
Russula aeruginea
Russula paludosa
Russula obscura
Russula olivacea
Russula aurata
Tricholoma gambosum, St George's
   Mushroom
Tricholoma columbetta
Tricholoma flavorirens
Tricholoma portentosum
Tricholoma cingulatum
Tricholoma argyraceum
Tricholoma irinum
Volvariella speciosa

Roots

Root vegetables are not too popular today, what with our affluent disdain for starchy fillers, and the heavy demands upon agricultural land for more profitable crops. Yet it is still surprising how very few edible wild tubers have been taken into cultivation. But at the time plant domestication was beginning to be taken seriously in this country, vegetables, including roots, had a rather soiled reputation. Being eaten by animals they hardly commended themselves to the meat-addicted middle classes. Nor did the poor think much of them as a substitute for bread. According to the dietary theory which happened to be current, they were looked on either as a potential source of wind and melancholy, or of diarrhoea. R. Burton, in his *Anatomy of Melancholy*, (1621) had this to say of them:

'The same Crato will allow no roots at all to be eaten. Some approve of potatoes, parsnips, but all corrected for wind.'

It was not until 1699, when John Evelyn wrote his bewitching, precocious book *Acetaria: a Discourse on Salletts* that an important writer stood up for vegetables in their own right, served fresh or cooked conservatively.

Consequently, roots tended to be domesticated for animal rather than human fodder, and no more than half a dozen of our wild tubers have been developed, directly or indirectly, into food plants.

It is not possible to make up completely for this deficiency by cashing in on the wild stock, as will be seen from the heavy preponderance of grade C entries in this section. There are two reasons for this bias. Firstly, the undesirability of tearing whole wild plants out of the ground. In public places this is quite rightly illegal. But even on private or waste ground it is not a practice to be encouraged except with the commonest species.

Secondly, few plants in the wild, (except perennials, whose

rootstocks live on from one year to the next) can afford to develop fleshy roots. Annuals, which live for only one season and depend for their continuance on the successful germination of their seeds, must concentrate all available food supplies into the seed production process. Those individuals that have a genetic tendency to divert this food into building up stocky roots, will usually produce small quantities of poor seed, and won't flourish as a breeding strain. If you look at the annual radish, for instance, a successful self-seeder in the wild, you will see that it has an almost completely unswollen root.

So in looking for plants with roots large enough to be eaten, go for the late flowerers, which are more likely to have built up a fleshy tuber.

Horseradish *Armoracia rusticana* [A]

Very common in waste ground in England and Wales; rare in Scotland and Ireland. Flowers from May to September, a shock of white blossoms on a long spike. Leaves: large, slightly toothed, and dock-like, growing straight up from the root stem to a height of about 3′.

There can scarcely be any other plant of such wide commercial use that is so neglected in the wild. Small jars of horseradish sauce sell for up to three shillings each, yet the plant grows untouched and in abundance on waste ground throughout England. British Rail could probably pay off their deficit if they cropped the plants growing along their cuttings.

The rougher the ground, the more horseradish seems to relish it. It will grow on derelict gardens, bomb sites, even abandoned brick piles. So you should have no trouble in finding a patch that no-one will object to your digging up.

There can be little mistaking its crinkly, palm-like leaves, but if you are in any doubt, crush them between your fingers: they should have the characteristic horseradish smell. A spade – desirable when gathering all roots – is imperative with horseradish. The plant is a perennial, and carries an extensive and complex root-system. You will need to dig quite deep and chop the woody structure to obtain a section for use.

The worst part of preparing horseradish is the peeling. Any

section will be intractably knobbly, and need considerable geometric skill before it can be reduced to a manageable shape. Once it has been, the remains of the brown outer layer should be pared off with a sharp knife.

You will be left with some pure white chunks of horseradish which need to be grated before they can be used. This is best done out of doors, as the fumes put the most blinding onions to shame.

The freshly-grated root can be used as it stands, as a garnish for roast beef. But use it fairly quickly, as it loses its potency in a few days. To make an instant sauce from it, whip it up with some plain yoghourt and a little sugar and seasoning. A more substantial and longer lasting sauce is made this way. Mix a teaspoon of dry mustard with a tablespoon of cold water, and blend until smooth. Combine with six heaped tablespoons of grated horseradish and salt and pepper. Allow to stand for a quarter of an hour. Then blend into a cupful of white sauce (or double cream if you do not want it to last especially long.)

For a rampaging alternative, try the Universal Devil's Mixture:

'To devil the same, rub each piece over with the following mixture, having made a deep incision in any article of food that may be subjected to this Mephistophelian process. Put in a bowl a good tablespoonful of Durham mustard which mix with four tablespoonsful of Chilli vinegar. Add to it a tablespoonful of grated horseradish, two bruised shallots, a teaspoonful of salt, half ditto of Cayenne, ditto of black pepper, and one of pounded sugar, two teaspoonsful of chopped chillies, if handy. Add the yolks of two raw eggs. Take a paste brush, and after having slightly seasoned each piece with salt, rub over each piece with the same, probing some into the incisions. First broil slowly and then the last few minutes as near as possible to the Pandemonium fire.'

From *The Culinary Campaign*, Alexis Soyer, 1857

Wild parsnip *Pastinaca sativa* [A]   **Pl. 2**

Local names: COW-CAKES, Scotland; COW-FLOP, KEGGAS, Corn.

Widespread and locally common in the South and East of England, in waste ground and grassy places, especially on chalk and limestone. Flowers July to October, in yellow umbels. Leaves:

usually 8-9 opposed on each leaf branch. The whole plant is hairy and grows to about 2′ to 4′ in height.

The wild parsnip is a stocky, economic plant, with none of the excess and luxuriance of some of our umbelliferae. In the poor soils of road verges and waste ground it often grows to no more than 18″ in height. Its chrome yellow umbels could only really be confused with those of fennel (see p. 126) which is instantly distinguishable by its feathery leaves and aniseed smell.

Pastinaca sativa is probably a direct ancestor of our cultivated parsnips. An experiment at Cirencester in the mid-19th century produced very large, fleshy roots directly from the wild stock in a space of ten years. No more was done than to transplant the wild parsnips into some rich garden soil, and to resow each season with the seeds of those with the largest roots.

The parsnip was almost certainly being cultivated as far back as the Middle Ages, as Gerard mentions the wild root with some distaste at a time when some form of parsnip figured very prominently in country recipes. Yet the Romans apparently did not bother to domesticate the plant, as Pliny complains of not being able to get rid of its rather pungent flavour.

The root of the wild parsnip, as well as being strongly flavoured, is also rather thin and wiry, in spite of being a biennial and having two years to grow from seed to flowering maturity. But if you concentrate on the late flowerers, and wait till the first frost before digging up their roots, you will find them both softened and sweetened. (You may need to mark them if the frosts are late, as the plants become understandably nondescript as the leaves start to brown.)

The parsnip was especially valued in historical times for its sweetness, and it figures in as many early recipes for sauces, cakes and puddings as it does in the form of a vegetable pure and simple. And this is a good way to use the wild variety, for however good the specimens you obtain, they will always have a hardy woody core.

The roots should be washed, peeled, and boiled in water until they are quite soft (about three-quarters of an hour). Then mash them and press them through a rough sieve to remove the fibrous parts. With the purée you can make a pie, or form it into cakes by mixing with flour, butter and spices, and frying. Alternatively you can make a parsnip sauce, traditionally served with cod, by reheating the purée with cream and a little butter rolled in flour. Heat and stir the mixture until it thickens, and season with salt and nutmeg.

Then again, there is nothing against using wild parsnips as vegetables, boiled or baked, provided you can take the flavour neat, and don't mind sucking them off the central core.

Dandelion *Taraxacum officinale* [A]

Local Names: very varied, including BUM-PIPE, BURNING FIRE, CLOCKS, CLOCK FLOWER, CLOCKS AND WATCHES, COMBS AND HAIRPINS, CONQUER MORE, DEVIL'S MILK-PLANT, DEVIL'S MILK-PAIL, DOG-POSY, FAIRY CLOCKS, FARMER'S CLOCKS, GOLDEN SUNS, HORSE GOWAN, IRISH DAISY, LAY A-BED, LION'S TEETH, MALE, MESS-A-BED, PISHAMOOLAG, PISS-A-BED, PISSIMIRE, PITTLE BED, PRIEST'S CROWN, SCHOOLBOY'S CLOCK, SHEPHERD'S CLOCK, SHIT-A-BED, STINK DAVINE, SWINE'S SNOUT, TELL-TIME, TIME FLOWER, TIME-TELLER, TWELVE O'CLOCK, WET-WEED, WISHES.

Widespread and abundant in open and grassy places throughout British Isles. Flowers February to November, but especially April and May. Largish golden-yellow flowers made up of numerous fine petals, on hollow stems up to one foot tall. Leaves grow from base of plant and are roughly toothed. The whole plant exudes a milky juice when cut.

The dandelion is one of the most profuse of British weeds, and in late spring is liable to cover almost any grassy place with

PLATE I

PLATE 2 (see p. 65 for identification)

PLATE 3 (see p. 80 for identification)

PLATE 4 (see p. 81 for identification)

its blazing yellow flowers. Its leaves – and consequently its roots – can be found at almost any time of the year except the very coldest, which is welcome, given the wide range of food uses to which the plant can be put.

The normal use of the long white roots is to make a coffee substitute, which is almost indistinguishable from real coffee, yet which lacks the possibly injurious stimulant, caffeine. Dig up the roots in the autumn, when they are at their fattest and most mellow, and scrub well (though do not peel). Dry them thoroughly, preferably in the sun, and then roast in an oven until they are brittle. Grind them fairly coarsely and use as ordinary coffee.

The Japanese use the root as a vegetable, cooked Nituke-style. Chop the scrubbed roots into thin rings. Sauté these in vegetable oil, using about one tablespoonful of oil to one cup of chopped roots. Then add a small amount of water, a little salt, and cover the pan. Stew until the roots are soft and most of the moisture and added water have evaporated. Finally add a dash of soya sauce.

The flowers of the dandelion make a well known wine, and the leaves are widely used as a salad herb (see p. 83).

White water-lily *Nymphaea alba* [C]   Pl. 2

This is the common water-lily found in sheltered ponds, waxy-white of flower and complicated of architecture. Its use as a source of food is an exemplary study of man's thoroughness in searching out improbable things to eat, for it is the *underground* tubers, sometimes six feet below the surface of the water, that have been eaten in Northern Europe.

PLATE 2   **Plants with Edible Roots**

Turnip *Brassica rapa* [C]

Brassica rapa is a close relative of the cultivated turnip and has been used as a source of human and animal food since pre-historic times. The plant is a biennial and produces quite large swollen roots even in the wild state. John Evelyn suggests making bread from them:

'Let the Turneps first be peel'd and boil'd in Water till soft and tender; then strongly pressing out the juice, mix them together, and when dry (beaten or pounded very fine) with their weight of Wheat-meal, season it as you do other bread, and knead it; then letting the dough remain a little to ferment, fashion the Paste into Loaves, and bake it like common bread.'

He goes on with a very modern barbecuish tip:

'Some roast turneps in a Pan under the Embers, and eat them with Sugar and Butter.' *Acetaria*

The young leaves, 'turnip tops', can be used as a green vegetable (see p. 102).

Radish *Raphanus sativus* [C]

This is not the true wild radish, *Raphanus raphanistrum*, but a variety of the cultivated form (sometimes crossed with the wild) that occurs occasionally as a casual or garden outcast.

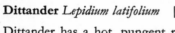

Dittander *Lepidium latifolium* [C]

Dittander has a hot, pungent root, and was gathered from the wild and occasionally grown in gardens as a condiment before horseradish and pepper became popular. It is a perennial and has an obstinate and aggressive root system like horseradish, yet is now uncommon in the wild. Only beside a few estuaries on the South and East coasts can the tall, elegant leaves still be found.

Spring beauty *Claytonia perfoliata* [C]

A curious and endearing little immigrant from America which was not observed in this country until the middle of the last century. It has leaves which totally encircle its smooth stems. The small, starchy bulbs were much prized by North American Indians.

Marsh mallow *Althaea officinalis* [C]

The plant that gave the sweet its name. Today marshmallow is made from starch, gelatine and sugar. But once it was produced from the roots of *Althaea officinalis*, which contain not only their own starch, but albumen, a crystallisable sugar, a fixed oil and a good deal of gelatinous matter. They were gathered by fishermen's wives in the dykes and saltmarshes of the East Coast, where the plant still grows, in soft-branched clumps with velvety pink flowers.

Rest-harrow *Ononis repens* [C]

A common enough plant in dry and chalky grassland, but too handsome to pick needlessly. It is like a sweet pea bred for the rockery: short, pert and bushy. The root is tough and serpentine. In the North children would dig it up and chew it; hence it acquired the names wild liquorice and spanish root.

Wild liquorice *Astragulus glycyphyllus* [C]   **Pl. 2**

Commercial liquorice is made from a relative of this plant (*Glycrrhiza glabra*) by pulping the roots and condensing the resultant juice. That this British plant was similarly named suggests that at one time it was similarly used - but I have found no record of this so far. It is a member of the vetch family, and grows locally on sunny banks on chalk and limestone.

Bitter vetch *Lathyrus montanus* [C]

Another edible tuber from the pea family. Bitter vetch is one of the commoner species, and sometimes grows in abundance in heathy areas. It has been recognised as a vegetable since at least

67

the Middle Ages, and Gerard, later likening the taste of the roots to chestnut, has some typically muted praise for it:

'The Nuts of this Pease being boiled and eaten, are hardlier digested then be either Turneps or Parsneps, yet they do nourish no less then the Parsneps: they are not so windie as they, they do more slowly passe thorowe the belly by reason of their binding qualitie, and being eaten rawe, they be yet harder of digestion, and do hardlier and slowlier descend.'   From *The Herbal*

In later times the roots have been used as a subsistence crop in the Scottish Islands, either raw or dried. They have also been used for flavouring whisky.

Dropwort *Filipendula vulgaris* [c]   Pl. 2

The meadowsweet of dry chalk and limestone downland. A delightfully contrasted plant with crisply cut leaflets, and soft, pink-tinged flowers.

The roots have been eaten on the continent, but are rather bitter.

Silverweed *Potentilla anserina* [c]   Pl. 2

An abundant flower of damp grassy and waste places. The undersides of the leaves are flashed with a pale matt grey, making the plant look withered before its time. Yet the tops are a silky, liquid green, and the leaves were once used by foot soldiers as an apparently cooling lining for their boots. The whole plant has a history of medicinal and culinary use going back to the Greeks.

The roots were cultivated as a crop from late prehistoric times. In the upland areas of Great Britain they were used right up until the introduction of the potato – and later, in times of famine. The roots were boiled or baked or even eaten raw, and the botanist John Ray likened their taste to parsnip. They were also dried and ground into flour for bread and gruel.

Silverweed is worth bringing into your garden for its ambivalent leaves and yellow, utilitarian flowers. If you do, some of those old famine recipes for the roots are worth reviving.

Herb bennet *Geum urbanum* [C]

The clove-like odour of the roots of herb bennet, or wood avens, was once reputed to repel moths; yet it clearly attracted human beings, for it was widely grown as a pot-herb in the sixteenth century. As well as its many medicinal uses (against 'the stings of venomous beasts') it was also added to broths and soups.

The wood avens is an undistinguished plant, yet it is pleasant in late summer to find its small 5-petalled yellow flowers on an otherwise dark woodland floor.

Large evening primrose *Oenothera erythrosepala* [C] **Pl. 2**

A tall, downy flower with a fine poppy-like yellow blossom. It was introduced from America into Britain in the early seventeenth century, and was soon taken into gardens for its roots, which were eaten boiled. In Germany the young shoots were also eaten.

Sea holly *Eryngium maritimum* [C] **Pl. 2**

A beautiful plant of the seashore which has suffered much for the sake of holidaymakers' vases. It is a thistle-like plant, its spiny, ice-blue leaves covered with bloom and ribbed and edged with a fine white tracery of veins. It likes the rough ground of sandy and shingly beaches, and its roots have consequently been confused more than once with those of the vitriolic horned poppy, with curious results:

'a certain person made a pye of the roots of this plant, supposing them to be the roots of the Eryngo, of which he had before eaten pyes which were very pleasant, and eating it while it was hot, became delirious, and having voided a stool in a white chamber pot, fancied it to be gold, breaking the pot in pieces, and desiring what he imagined as gold might be preserved as such. Also his man and maid servant eating of the same pye, fancied of what they saw to be gold.'

> Philosophical Transactions, 1698
> quoted in *The Englishman's Flora*

Sea holly roots, as Eryngo roots, were once extensively used for making candied sweetmeats. The roots were dug up (they could be up to six feet long) in the spring or autumn, partly boiled until they could be peeled and then cut into thin slices. These were cooked with an equal weight of sugar until the latter became syrup, when the roots were removed and allowed to cool.

Candied Eryngo roots were a vital ingredient of that redoubtable Elizabethan dish, marrow-bone pie.

Pignut *Conopodium majus* [C]

The custom of grubbing for pig or earth nuts seems to have died out now, even amongst children. There was a time when they were one of the most popular of wayside nibbles, even though extracting them from the ground was as delicate a business as an egg and spoon race. They cannot be pulled out, for the thin leaf stalk breaks off very quickly. The fine white roots must be unearthed with a knife, and carefully traced down to the tuber.

The 'nuts' can be eaten raw, once they have been scraped or washed, though one early botanist recommended them peeled and boiled in broth with pepper. The plant, a slender, feathery umbellifer, is still common in June and July in woods, meadows and sandy heaths.

Spignel-meu *Meum athamanticum* [C]

In the Highlands, where spignel meu occasionally appears on hill pastures, the roots of this rare umbelliferate have been eaten like parsnips.

The whole plant is highly aromatic, to the extent of giving a sweet scent to the milk of cows which graze on its foliage.

Rampion *Campanula rapunculus* [C]

Now an exceedingly rare plant, the rampion must once have been much commoner in this country, for it figures widely in recipes up to the seventeenth century. All parts of the plant were eaten. The thick, fleshy roots were chopped, boiled and served with vinegar, and the young leaves used as a salad herb.

70

Ox-eye daisy *Chrysanthemum leucanthemum* [c]

John Evelyn reported that the roots of this, our commonest large daisy, were eaten as a salad vegetable in Spain.

Chicory *Cichorium intybus* [c]

The 'succory' of the old herbalists, a tall, distinguished plant with startling cornflower-blue blossoms. Chicory is probably not a native of the British Isles, but it still grows in quite a wide range of grassy habitats, especially on chalk and limestone.

The roots are boiled and eaten by the Arabs, and it is from the Arabic *Chicouryeh* that the English name for the plant is derived. Roast and ground, the roots make an acceptable (though slightly bitter) substitute for, or addition to, coffee, and have been extensively cultivated for this purpose.

The leaves of the plant are used as a salad vegetable (see p. 84).

Flowering rush *Butomus umbellatus* [c]   **Pl. 2**

The bulbs of this handsome aquatic plant are edible. The flowering rush grows locally in fresh water and its tall stems are topped in the summer by inch-wide rose-pink flowers.

Galingale *Cyperus longus* [c]

Galingale was one of the favourite spices of the medieval kitchen. It was used in soups and pies and sweets with the same abandon as saffron and ginger. There has always been some confusion amongst scholars about what precisely this spice is, and a number, no doubt because of its Latin name, have falsely equated it with the ground root of the cypress pine. It is in fact derived from the tubers of a rush which grows in a few moist places in the Southwest.

Cyperus longus has never been common in Britain, and the variety used in early cooking was probably the sub-species *Cyperus esculentus*, which was imported from the Mediterranean.

Galingale is almost impossible to obtain now, but it was an ingredient in an enormous number of delightful dishes. One of them, pokerounce, was a sort of medieval cinnamon toast, and is delicious without the galingale.

A pot of honey was well baked and then mixed with ginger, cinnamon and galingale. The resulting paste was spread on to hot buttered toast, and the whole garnished with pine nuts.

Salsify *Tragopogon porrifolius* [c]

Salsify was one of the unhappy casualties of the contraction in our taste for vegetables which occurred in the first half of this century. Its extraordinary flavour may be partly the cause, since it tastes more like baked salt fish than a root vegetable. It still grows wild in a few places, chiefly near estuaries in the South East of England. It is a tall, straight plant, with purplish dandelion-like flowers.

Although picking the wild specimens is not to be encouraged whilst the plant is still so uncommon, it ought to be purchased more often from the few greengrocers which stock the cultivated variety. The long white roots are first carefully peeled, and then boiled or steamed with butter and lemon juice. The flavour is sufficiently individual for the roots to be served as a dish on their own.

Common star of Bethlehem *Ornithogalum umbellatum* [c] **Pl. 2**

A beautiful, pure white flower of the lily family, which grows locally in grassy places, mainly in East Anglia. It was introduced into America where it is now abundant in many places. The bulbs are cooked and eaten there as well as in the Middle East.

Early purple orchis *Orchis mascula* [c]

It would be criminal to dig up any of the dwindling colonies of British orchids, let alone for food. Yet I felt I must include this lilac flowered woodland species for completeness' sake, as it has been one of the most fascinating and valuable of all wild foods. The tubers contain a starch-like substance called bassorine, which has in it more nutritive matter than any other single plant product, one ounce being sufficient to sustain a man for a whole day.

In the Middle East, where the plant is more common, it is still widely used. The roots are dug up after the plant has flowered, and are occasionally eaten as they stand, either raw or cooked. But they are most usually made into a drink called Cahlab. For this the tubers are dried in the sun and ground into a rough flour. This is mixed with honey and cinnamon, and stirred into hot milk until it thickens.

In Britain, a similar drink called Salop was a common soft drink long before the introduction of coffee houses. In Victorian books it is frequently mentioned as a tea-break beverage of manual workers. They made it with water more often than with milk, sometimes lacing it with spirits, sometimes brewing it so thick that it had to be eaten with a spoon.

Perhaps the lustier concoctions were a product of the plant's legendary reputation as an aphrodisiac, which dates back to classical times ('orchis' means testicle, referring to the shape of the twin tubers). In the more fruitful days of the seventeenth century one botanist was moved to remark that enough orchids grew in Cobham Park to pleasure all the seamen's wives in Rochester. And a body as august as the College of Physicians published this astonishing recipe in their Pharmacopoeia as 'a Provocative to Venery'. It would most certainly move the bowels if not the loins.

Orchid tubers, dates, bitter almonds, Indian nuts, pine nuts, pistachio nuts, candied ginger, candied Eryngo root, clover, galingale, peppers, ambergris, musk, penids (barley sugar), cinnamon, saffron, Malaga wine, nutmeg, mace, grains of Paradise, ash-keys, the 'belly and loins of scinks', borax, benzoine, wood of aloes, cardamons, nettle seed, and avens root.

(Quoted in *The Englishman's Flora* by Geoffrey Grigson)

Lords and ladies *Arum maculatum* [C]   Pl. 2

A plant most country children are wisely taught to beware of. It grows abundantly in the shade of hedgerows and woods, like so many painted china ornaments. It is a plant which appears in several deceptively attractive disguises. The glossy, arrow-

73

shaped leaves are amongst the very first foliage to appear in late winter. They are followed by a paler green cowl, which encloses the club-shaped flower. In late summer the hood withers and the flower produces a spike of shiny orange berries. All these stages and parts produce in the raw state an acrid, burning juice, which is a serious irritant both internally and externally. The root also contains this poisonous element; yet if it is well baked it is completely harmless. The cooked and ground roots were once in demand in this country under the name Portland sago, since the trade was centred round the Isle of Portland. The powder was used like Salop (see p. 73) or as a substitute for arrowroot.

Green Vegetables

There are an enormous number of edible green leaves – probably many more than I have been able to trace for this book. To make this section a little less cumbersome, I have therefore divided it into four categories of 'greens': those that are commonly used raw, as salad vegetables; those that are cooked like spinach; those whose stems are the part which is usually eaten; and seaweeds. But these divisions are fairly arbitrary. Any plant whose stem is edible also has edible leaves; any plant normally eaten raw is likely to be just as useful cooked.

The main problem with wild leaf vegetables is their *size*. Not many wild plants have the big, floppy leaves for which cultivated greens have been bred, and as a result picking enough for a serving can be a long and back-breaking task. For this reason the optimum picking time for most leaf vegetables is probably their middle-age, when the flowers are out and the plant is easy to recognise, and the leaves have reached maximum size without beginning to wither.

Salad Herbs

Watercress *Rorippa nasturtium-aquaticum*   [A]   **Pl. 3**

Local names: BILDERS, E. Ang; BROOKLIME, Bucks; CAR-PENTER'S CHIPS, Glos; CREESE, Som; TANG-TONGUES, Yks; TONGUE-GRASS, Ire; WATER-GRASS, N. Ire; WELL-GIRSE, Scot.

Grows abundantly in and by running water throughout the British Isles. Flowers from June to October in a bunch of small white blossoms. Stem hollow and creeping; leaves a rich, silky green.

Now reduced to a steak-house garnish, watercress was once one of our most respected green vegetables. It was certainly under small scale cultivation by the middle of the eighteenth century, and quickly became a commercial product as the fast growing science of nutrition caught a glimpse of its anti-scorbutic properties (which result, as we know now, from an exceptionally high Vitamin C content). Henry Mayhew has some fascinating notes on the watercress trade:

'The first coster-cry heard of a morning in the London streets is of 'Fresh wo-orter-creases'. Those that sell them have to be on their rounds in time for the mechanic's breakfast, or the day's gains are lost. . . . At the principal entrance to Farringdon market there is an open space, running the entire length of the railings in front and extending from the iron gates at the entrance to the sheds down the centre of the large paved court before the shops. In this open space the cresses are sold, by the salesmen or saleswomen to whom they are consigned, in the hampers they are brought in from the country. . . . The market – by the time we reach it – has just begun; one dealer has taken his seat, and sits motionless with cold – for it wants but a month to Christmas – with his hands thrust deep into the pockets of his gray driving coat. Before him is an opened hamper with a candle fixed in the centre of the bright green cresses, and as it shines through the wicker sides of the basket, it casts curious patterns on the ground – as a night shade does. Two or three customers, with their "shallows" slung over their backs, and their hands poked into the bosoms of their gowns, are bending over the hampers, the light from which tinges their swarthy features, and they rattle their halfpence and speak coaxingly to the dealer to hurry him in their bargains. . . . Even by the time the cress market is over it is yet so early that the maids are beating the mats in the road, and mechanics, with their tool baskets slung over their shoulders are still hurrying to their work.'

From *London Labour and the London Poor*, 1851

Most of the watercress we eat today is grown commercially; but the cultivated plants are identical in every respect to those that grow wild, sometimes in great green hillocks, on the muddy edges of almost all freshwater streams.

The plants to pick are not the young ones, which are rather tasteless, but the older, sturdier specimens, whose darker leaves have a slight burnish to them. These are the tangy ones, which justify the plant's Latin name, *Nasi-tortium* (meaning 'nose-twisting'). Never pick watercress from stagnant water, or streams

which flow through pastureland. The eggs of the liver fluke –
equally at home inside humans and sheep – have a liking for
the hollow stems.

Do not pull the plants up by the root, but cut the tops of the
shoots, and wash well whatever environment you have picked them
in. The sprigs can be used in almost any sort of salad. They are
especially good with nuts, and with oranges and lemons. Remember
that watercress is improved with a little salt. It can also be
stewed as a green vegetable, or simmered with mashed pickled
walnuts as a tart sauce for boiled fish.

The following common members of the cabbage family all have
the spicy flavour of watercress, and can be used in much the
same way.

White mustard *Sinapis alba* [B]

A common weed in arable land, especially on chalky soils.
Flowers May to October. This is the mustard of 'mustard and
cress'. Under cultivation the plants are picked when they are only
a few inches high. In the wild they need to be picked rather later
for positive identification, by which time they tend to be slightly
bitter.

Common penny cress *Thlaspi arvense* [B]

A widespread and common plant of arable and waste places.
Flowers May to November.

Lady's smock *Cardamine pratensis* [B]

Common in damp meadows, woods and by the edges of rivers.
Flowers April to June.

Hairy bittercress *Cardamine hirsuta* [B]

Common and widespread on rocks, dunes, stony gardens and
other bare places. Flowers March to September. A pleasantly
tangy plant, fleshier and sweeter than watercress.

77

Common winter cress *Barbarea vulgaris* [B]

Widespread by the sides of roads and streams. Flowers May to July. Used to be called land-cress to distinguish it from the winter cress of commerce, which is a sub-species of watercress. It is occasionally sold in markets in the United States, where it is often cooked as well as being used as an ingredient of salads.

Jack-by-the-hedge *Alliaria petiolata* [A]   **Pl. 3**

Local names: HEDGE GARLIC, GARLIC MUSTARD. BEGGAR-MAN'S OATMEAL, Leic; LADY'S NEEDLEWORK, LAMB'S PUMMY, Som; PENNY-HEDGE, Norf, Worc; PICK- POCKET, Dev; POOR MAN'S MUSTARD, Lincs; SAUCE ALONE, Som.

Widespread and plentiful at the edges of woods and on hedge banks. Flowers April to June, small, brilliantly white flowers. Leaves: a fresh, bright green, and slightly toothed. Height 1' to 3'.

Welcome previews of the spring, the soft leaves of hedge garlic can sometimes be seen as early as February if there has been a mild winter. If a warm autumn follows there is often a second crop of stubby, flowerless shoots in September and October.

For those who like garlic, but only in moderation, Jack-by-the-hedge is ideal as a flavouring. When bruised or chopped the leaves give off just a suspicion of the smell of its unrelated namesake. Yet one Dr Prior, in *Popular Names of British Plants*, clearly thought otherwise when he gave this bizarre explanation for the common name of the plant:

'Jack or Jakes, latrina, alluding to its offensive smell.'

Jack-by-the-hedge is a pleasant plant, upright, balanced in colouring and classically simple in construction, and only a few leaves should be picked from each specimen. Some of the local names show that the kitchen use of the leaves has a long history. Turner mentions it, and Gerard suggests it as a sauce for fish.

It is useful finely chopped in salads, but best possibly as a sauce for lamb, especially valley lamb which may well have fed on it in low lying pastures. In the early spring, chop the leaves with hawthorn buds and a little mint, mix well with vinegar and sugar, and serve with the lamb as you would a mint sauce.

Lime *Tilia europaea* [A]   **Pl. 3**

Local names: LINDEN

Common in parks, by roadsides and in ornamental woods and
copses. Flowers in July, a drooping cluster of heavily scented
yellow blossoms (see p. 150). Leaves, large and heart-shaped,
smooth above, paler below with a few tufts of fine white hairs.
The lime is a tall tree when it is allowed to grow naturally, with
a smooth, dark brown trunk usually interrupted by a few bosses.

The common lime is a cultivated hybrid between our two
uncommon species of wild, native lime. A few have escaped to
grow naturally in woodland, but the majority are to be found
in fairly formal settings, in the places they were set down by the
landscapers. No doubt the latter's intentions were the stately
lines of trees that have indeed matured in a few estates. But the
modern municipal planner's obsession with prissy tidiness has
had the limes snipped back annually till they look like withered
shaving brushes.

Still, the leaves thrive under this treatment, and no tree will
suffer any additional indignity if you pinch a few to munch on
the way home. They are thick, cooling, and very glutinous.
In high summer, before they begin to roughen, they make a
sandwich filling in their own right, between thin slices of new
white bread, unsalted butter and just a sprinkling of lemon juice
or Worcester sauce. Cut off the stalks and wash well, but otherwise
put them between the bread as they come off the tree.

Wood-sorrel *Oxalis acetosella* [A]   **Pl. 3**

Local names: Abundant, including: HALLELUJAH, BREAD-
AND-CHEESE, BUTTER AND EGGS, CUCKOO'S MEAT, FAIRY
BELLS, FOX'S MEAT, GOD ALMIGHTY'S BREAD-AND-CHEESE,
GOOD LUCK, GREEN SAUCE, GREEN SOB, KING FINGER,
LAVEROCKS, SALT CELLAR, SOUR SAB, WHITSUN FLOWER,
WILD SHAMROCK.

Widespread and common throughout the British Isles in woods
and other shady places. Flowers April to May, five white petals
on a delicate stem. Leaves shamrock-shaped, and lime green
when young. 2″ to 4″ high.

On the dark, barren floors of conifer woods, the leaves of the wood sorrel – often the only plant growing there in the spring – can look an almost luminous viridian. They lie in scattered clusters amongst the needles, like fretwork. Gerard Manley Hopkins described the new leaves of the plant as having the sharp appearance of green lettering. They are folded to begin with, in the shape of some episcopal hat, then open flat, three hearts with their points joined at the stem.

Wood sorrel was being used as a salad vegetable certainly as early as the fourteenth century. By the fifteenth it was under cultivation, and later John Evelyn recommended it in a list of plants suitable for kitchen gardens.

Its use then was an ingredient for salads, or pulped as a sharpening ingredient for sauces. It can be used the same way today, but sparingly, since it contains certain oxalates which are not too good for the body in large quantities. It is these salts which are responsible for the plant's pleasantly sharp taste, which is not unlike the skins of grapes.

The American Indians apparently fed the roots of this plant to their horses to increase their speed.

The following leaves are all useful as small scale additions to salads.

Wild strawberry *Fragaria vesca* [B]   **Pl. 3**

Widespread and common in heaths, grassy places and woodland rides. Flowers April to July.

A substantial, furry-tasting leaf, not at all sharp.

Parsley piert *Aphanes arvensis* [B]

Widespread and common on arable and dry ground.
Flowers April to October.

The curious name of this plant probably derives from *perce-pierre*, a plant which breaks through stony ground. So, by sympathetic magic, it came to be used medicinally as a specific against kidney stones. Yet it was Culpeper of all people, herbal wizard extraordinary, who first recommended it as an honest domestic pickle.

Salad burnet *Poterium sanguisorbum* [B]

Quite common in grassy places on chalk. Flowers May to August.

When crushed the leaves of the salad burnet smell slightly of cucumber. They have long been used as an ingredient of salads, in spite of their diminutive size, and as a garnish for cooling summer drinks.

Brooklime *Veronica beccabunga* [B]

Widespread and common by the edges of streams and in wet places. Flowers May to September.

A quite widely used salad plant in North Europe, which to my taste is rather bitter. Yet the American sub-species was actually praised by *Scientific American*: 'A salad plant equal to the watercress. Delightful in flavour, healthful and anti-scorbutic.'

F.F.—F

Cornsalad *Valerianelle locusta* [B]

Quite common in arable ground, on banks and walls. Flowers April to July.

A useful plant which continues to leaf throughout the winter.

Hawthorn *Crataegus monogyna* [A] **Pl. 3**

Local names: Numerous, including AZZY-TREE, BREAD-AND-CHEESE TREE, HAGTHORN, HOLY INNOCENTS, MAY, MOON FLOWER, QUICKTHORN, WHITETHORN.

Widespread and abundant in heaths, downs, hedges, scrubland, light woods and all open land. Flowers May to June, abundant umbels of white (sometimes pink), strongly scented blossoms. Leaves deeply lobed on spiny branches. Whole shrub up to 20′ high.

The 'Bread and Cheese' of the young leaf shoots is probably the first wild vegetable a country schoolchild eats. The name is scarcely appropriate, since the leaves taste nothing whatever like bread and cheese. Yet a number of edible wild plants have this amongst their local names, and it is probably a metaphor for their basic food value rather than a description of their taste.

Either way the very young leaves, picked in April, have a pleasantly nutty taste, and are an excellent addition to oily salads. The buds can be picked much earlier in the year, though it takes an age to gather any quantity, and they tend to fall apart anyway. There is a splendid recipe for a spring pudding which makes use of the leaf buds; but I would save your energy for the eating, and use the larger and more plentiful young leaf shoots.

Make a light suet crust, well-seasoned, and roll it out thinly and as long in shape as possible. Cover the surface with the young leaves, and push them slightly into the suet. Take some rashers of bacon, cut into fine strips and lay them across the leaves. Moisten the edges of the dough and roll it up tightly, sealing the edges as you go. Tie in a cloth and steam for at least an hour. Cut it in thick slices like a Swiss roll, and serve with plenty of gravy.

Beech *Fagus sylvatica* [A]

(For details, see NUTS, p. 33)

In April the young leaves of the beech tree are almost trans-lucent. They shine in the sun from the light passing through them. To touch they are silky, and tear like delicately thin rubber. It is difficult not to want to chew a few as you walk through a beech-wood in spring. And, fresh from the tree, they are indeed a fine salad vegetable, as sweet as a mild cabbage though much softer in texture.

A more unusual way of utilising them is to make a potent liqueur, called beech leaf noyau. This probably originated in the Chilterns, where large plantations of beech were put down in the eighteenth and nineteenth centuries to service the chair-making trade.

Pack an earthenware or glass jar about nine tenths full of young, clean leaves. Pour gin into the jar, pressing the leaves down all the time, until they are just covered. Leave to steep for about a fortnight. Then strain off the gin, which will by now have caught the brilliant green of the leaves. To every pint of gin add about three-quarters of a pound of sugar (more if you like your liqueurs very syrupy) dissolved in half a pint of boiling water, and a dash of brandy. Mix well and bottle as soon as cold.

The result is a thickish, sweet spirit, mild and slightly oily to taste, like sake, but devastating in its effects!

Dandelion *Taraxacum officinale* [A]   **Pl. 3**

(For details, see ROOTS p. 65)

Dandelion leaves have the distinction of having been recom-mended by the Radio Doctor (Charles Hill) during one of his wartime 'Kitchen Front' broadcasts. His advice seemed to have little effect on the number of dandelion-eaters, which is a shame, for the plant is rich in minerals, and pleasantly bracing to eat. It has a long tradition of medicinal and culinary use, and culti-vated varieties have been developed in both the United States and France.

It is especially useful as a salad plant, since the leaves can be gathered at almost any time of the year. Only after prolonged frost or snow is it impossible to find any. Choose the youngest leaves and strip them from the plant by hand. The root is quite strong enough to be unaffected by this sort of picking. (If you have dandelions growing in your garden, try manuring them and covering the lower parts of the leaves with earth, to blanch them like chicory. They did this in medieval gardens and produced gigantic plants as a result.)

When you have sufficient leaves, trim off any excess stalk, and wash well. The roughly chopped leaves can be made into a good salad simply by dressing with olive oil, lemon juice and a trace of garlic. They can also be served in sandwiches with a dash of Worcester sauce, or cooked with butter like spinach.

Pissenlit au lard is a dandelion dish sometimes served in French restaurants. It consists of small pieces of crispy fried bacon, served hot on a raw dandelion salad base, and dressed with vinegar, bacon fat and seasoning. For extra colour and a new texture, throw in a few of the flower heads as well.

(The French name, and some of the English local names given on p. 64, should warn you that the plant has a small reputation as a diuretic.)

The following common plants, all members of the family which includes the dandelion, can have their leaves used in salads in similar ways.

Chicory *Cichorium intybus* [B]

Widespread throughout England and Wales, but only locally common, usually in grassy and waste places on chalk. Flowers June to September.

This is the plant which, after an extraordinarily complicated cultivation process, yields the cigar-shaped heads of chicory you buy in shops. (See also ROOTS p. 71).

Nipplewort *Lapsana communis* [B]

Widespread and common on shady banks, roadsides, etc. Flowers from June to September.

Catsear *Hypochoeris radicata* [B]

Common in dry pastures, open woods and other grassy places. Flowers May to September, but the leaves continue to grow through much of the winter.

Rough hawkbit *Leontodon hispidus* [B]

Common in meadows, roadside verges and dry, grassy places. Flowers May to September.

Goatsbeard *Tragopogon pratensis* [B]

Widespread and common in dry grassy places. Flowers June to September. (The roots have also been eaten.)

Wall lettuce *Mycelis muralis* [B]

Widespread but rather local on rocks, walls and other stony places. Flowers July to September.

Greater prickly lettuce *Lactuca virosa* [B]

Widespread in the South-East only, on chalky soils, especially near the sea. Flowers July to September.

This species is probably one of the ancestors of the cultivated lettuce, and is very tender to eat.

Corn sow-thistle *Sonchus arvensis* [B]   **Pl. 3**

Widespread and common throughout the British Isles, on road verges and cultivated ground. Flowers July to October.

Opinions are uncommonly divided about the virtues of this plant. Pliny has Theseus dining off a dish of sow-thistles before going to finish off the Minotaur. Later writers often use the name 'hare's lettuce', and describe how the hare, 'when fainting with the heat, she recruits her strength with this herb'. John Ray, usually the enthusiastic one, simply dismisses it: 'We leave it to be masticated by hares and rabbits.' For me it is the best of all these members of the daisy family, fleshier and milder than dandelion. But you must trim off the bristles at the edge of the leaves before use.

Garden cress *Lepidium sativum*   [C]

The cress of 'mustard and cress', which occurs occasionally in the wild as an escape. Like the mustard, it is sold commercially when only a few inches high.

Common scurvy-grass *Cochlearia officinalis*   [C]

Once famous as the major source of Vitamin C on long sea voyages. It was taken on board in the form of dried bundles or distilled extracts. But it is an unpleasantly bitter plant, and the taste was often disguised with spices.

But sailors were not the only ones with reason to fear scurvy, and fads for early morning scurvy-grass drinks, and scurvy-grass sandwiches abounded right up till the middle of the nineteenth century. It was only the ready availability of citrus fruits which finally made the plant obsolete.

Scurvy-grass still grows abundantly round cliffs and banks near the sea, and it was probably its convenient proximity that made it the favourite maritime anti-scorbutic. It is a rather nondescript little plant, no more than 9″ high, with small white flowers and dark-green heart-shaped leaves.

Golden saxifrage *Chrysosplenium oppositifolium* [c] **Pl. 3**

The golden saxifrage is a low, creeping plant with a preference for the banks of springs and wet, shady mountainsides. In the Vosges mountains the leaves are eaten under the name *Cresson de roches*.

Wintergreen *Pyrola minor* [c] **Pl. 3**

The plant of the liniment. Both the fruit and leaves of this evergreen bush are spicy and aromatic. The young, tender leaves are popular in America as a salad vegetable, and as the source of a tea.

The firm red berries hang on the stems all winter, and are wolfed by game birds. In America, those that are left in the spring are sold for pies. In Britain the plant is rather less abundant, but can be locally frequent in conifer woods and moors in the North.

Yarrow *Achillea millefolium* [c] **Pl. 3**

A sturdy, ferny plant that grows in abundance in grassy places, sometimes flowering right up to Christmas. Yarrow had a great reputation amongst herbalists as an astringent for wounds. Used in small quantities it can make a cool if rather bitter addition to salads. It can also be used as a cooked vegetable by removing the feathery leaves from the tough stems, boiling for twenty minutes, straining off the water, and then simmering in butter.

Greens

Sea beet *Beta vulgaris* [A]   **Pl. 4**

Local names: SEA SPINACH, WILD SPINACH.

Common on banks and shingle by the sea, except in Scotland.
Flowers June to September, tiny green blossoms in long leafy
spikes. Grows up to 3′ high with shiny, fleshy leaves.

One of the happy exceptions to the small-leaved tendency
among wild vegetables. Some of the bottom leaves of the sea
beet can grow as large and as heavy as those of any cultivated
spinach, and creak like parchment when you touch them.

This plant is the direct ancestor of all our cultivated beets,
from beetroots and mangolds through to chards and garden
spinach. Cultivation was probably begun at least 2000 years ago
in the Middle East and was mostly directed towards filling out
the long tap root into the forms we now pickle, feed to cattle
or turn into sugar. If you look closely at some of the wild species
you will occasionally find a red-veined individual that is no doubt
of the stock that was developed into the beetroot.

The leaves have scarcely been changed at all by cultivation and
I have yet to meet anyone who has eaten both wild and domestic
varieties who does not agree that the cultivated gains in size and
softness are outweighed by the loss in flavour.

You will be able to pick the leaves between April and October,
big, fleshy ones from the base of the plant and thinner, spear-
shaped ones near the head. Try and strip the larger leaves from
their central spine as you pick them; it will save much time during
preparation for cooking.

Always take special care in washing wild spinach leaves. The
bushy clumps they grow in are often the only prominent vegetation along coastal paths and sea walls, and are ideal targets for
perambulating dogs. Remove also the miscellaneous herbage

you will inevitably have grubbed up whilst picking the leaves, and the more substantial stems.

Wild spinach can be used in identical ways to the garden variety. The small leaves which grow on specimens very close to the sea are often as much as a sixteenth of an inch thick, and are ideal for salads. The larger ones should be boiled briskly in a large saucepan with not more than half an inch of water. Leave the lid on for a few minutes, and at intervals chop and press down the leaves. When all the vegetable has changed colour to a very dark green, remove the lid altogether and simmer for a further five minutes. Then transfer the spinach to a colander, and press out as much liquid as possible (saving it for gravies, stocks, etc). Return the greens to the saucepan, and toss over a low heat with a knob of butter. Some good additions to spinach cooked in this way are diced tomatoes and grated nuts.

The most intriguing recipe I know for spinach is for a seventeenth century spinach tart. Boil up the spinach in the usual way, and chop it up with a few hard-boiled egg yolks. Set into a pastry tart case, and pour on a sauce made of melted sugar, raisins and a touch of cinnamon. Bake in a moderate oven for about half an hour.

Fat-hen *Chenopodium album* [A]

Local names: ALL GOOD, Hants; BACON WEED, Dor; CONFETTI, Som; DIRTWEED, Som, Lincs; DIRTY DICK, Wilts, Ches; DOCK FLOWER, Som; DUNGWEED, Glos; LAMB'S QUARTERS, Som, IoW, N. Eng; MELDWEED, Scot; MUCK-HILL WEED, War; MUTTON CHOPS, Dor; MYLES, Berw; PIG WEED, Som, Hants; RAG JACK, Ches; WILD SPINACH, Midlands.

Abundant in cultivated and waste ground throughout British Isles. Flowers June to September. An undistinguished plant, up to three feet tall, with stiff upright stems and diamond-shaped leaves. Flowers: pale green, minute and bunched into spikes.

Fat hen is one of those plants that thrives in the company of humans. Prepare a manure heap in your garden and fat hen will doubtless begin to grow there within a few months. It is one of the very first plants to colonise ground that has been disturbed by roadworks or housebuilding, its stiff, mealy spikes often appearing in prodigious quantity. Wherever man is settling in, changing the landscape, fat hen will be there. No wonder then that its use as a food plant dates back to prehistoric times. Remains of the plant have been found in Neolithic settlements all over Europe. The seeds also formed part of the last, ritual gruel fed to Tollund Man (the man whose perfectly preserved corpse, stomach contents included, was recovered from a bog in Denmark in 1950).

In Anglo-Saxon times the plant was apparently of sufficient importance to have villages named after it. As *melde* it gave its name to Melbourn in Cambridgeshire, and Milden in Suffolk. The introduction of spinach largely put an end to the use of the plant, but its leaves continued to be eaten in Ireland and the Scottish Islands for a long while, and in many parts of Europe during the famine conditions of the last war. It has recently transpired that early people were lucky in this fortuitous choice of a staple vegetable: it contains more iron and protein than either cabbage or spinach, and more Vitamin B1 and calcium than raw cabbage.

It should be prepared and cooked in exactly the same way as spinach.

Spinach and fat-hen are the models for all cooked green vegetables, and the leaves of a number of plants in the same family can be used in the ways described above. As with all fodder-type vegetables, it is probably prudent not to eat large quantities regularly.

Good King Henry *Chenopodium bonus-henricus* [B]

Widespread but rather local by roadsides and in cultivated ground. Flowers May to August.

Another food plant of great antiquity, the remains of which have been found in Neolithic encampments. In medieval and Elizabethan times it was occasionally taken into cultivation. I have heard reports that it is making a comeback commercially, being sold at exorbitant prices from some city markets. An ironic fate for a prehistoric staple and a twentieth century weed.

Common orache *Atriplex patula* [B]

Widespread and abundant throughout the British Isles, in bare and waste ground. Flowers July to September.

Hastate orache *Atriplex hastata* [B]

Frequent throughout the British Isles, especially near the sea. Flowers July to September.

Sea purslane *Halimione portulacoides* [B]

Common on saltmarshes in the south and east of England. Flowers July to October.

The oval, fleshy leaves of this maritime plant make a succulent addition to salads.

Chickweed *Stellaria media* [B]   **Pl. 4**

Local names: CHICKWITTLES, Suff; CLUCKENWEED, N'thum; MISCHIEVOUS JACK, Som; MURREN, Yks; SKIRT BUTTONS, Dor; TONGUE-GRASS, Ire; WHITE BIRD'S EYE, Bucks.
Widespread and abundant throughout the British Isles in gardens and disturbed ground. Flowers throughout the year, a tiny, white, star-like flower, with five deeply divided petals. A weak plant which tends to straggle and creep before it has reached any height. It has single lines of fine hairs up alternate sides of the stem. Leaves: bright green and soft.

Chickweed must, after bindweed, be the gardener's most hated weed. Tons of it are incinerated every year. Yet it is one of the most deliciously tender of all wild vegetables. Gerard prescribed it for 'little birdes in cadges . . . when they loath their meate'. But even in his time it was cooked as a green vegetable, and later hawked around city streets by itinerant vegetable sellers.

Next time you are weeding, try saving the chickweed instead of burning it. Those without gardens should be able to find some by any field edge, even in the winter months. The leaves are too small to be picked individually, so strip bunches of the whole plant; the stems are just as tender to eat as the leaves. (But avoid confusion with the stiff, hairy mouse-ear chickweed, and the smooth, upright, red-stemmed petty spurge, which has a slight superficial resemblance to *Stellaria media*.)

Wash the sprigs well, and put into a saucepan without any additional water. Add a knob of butter, seasoning, and some chopped spring onions. Simmer gently for about ten minutes, turning all the time. Finish off with a dash of lemon juice or a sprinkling of grated nutmeg. Cooked this way chickweed is especially good with rich meat.

The following is a list of those small-leaved plants whose young shoots and leaves can be employed like chickweed, (though few of them come up to its quality).

Shepherds purse *Capsella bursa-pastoris* [B]

Abundant and widespread in waste and cultivated places. Flowers throughout the year.

A little like cabbage, though rather spicier. Popular in China, where it is sold in the markets.

Bladder campion *Silene vulgaris* [B]

Widespread and common by roadsides and in grassy places throughout the British Isles. Flowers June to August.

Rose bay *Epilobium angustifolium* [B]

Widespread and abundant on waste ground, heaths, woodland clearings, especially where there has been fire. Flowers June to September.

Linnaeus recommended the young leaves, and they are still used in some parts of Canada and Northern Europe.

Hogweed, Cow parsnip *Heracleum sphondylium* [B]

Widespread and abundant in hedges and grassy places. Flowers June to December.

The young shoots are marvellously fleshy.

Hop *Humulus lupulus* [B]

Locally frequent in hedges and damp thickets in England and Wales. Flowers July to August.

The very young shoots and leaves of the hop, picked not later than May, were probably in currency as a vegetable even before the flowers began to be used in brewing in the late Middle Ages (see FLOWERS, p. 153). They have been used chopped with butter as a sauce, and to fill out spring soups.

Yellow archangel *Galeobdolon luteum* [B]   **Pl. 4**

Widespread and locally common in woods and shady hedgerows in England and Wales. Flowers May to June.

Henbit *Lamium amplexicaule* [B]

Locally common throughout the British Isles, in cultivated ground. Flowers April to August.

93

Red dead-nettle *Lamium purpureum* [B]
Widespread and abundant in cultivated ground. Flowers throughout the year.

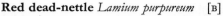

White dead-nettle *Lamium album* [B]

Widespread and common in hedgebanks, waste places, etc. Flowers March to September.

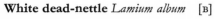

Common mallow *Malva sylvestris* [A]   **Pl. 4**

Local names: BILLY BUTTONS, Som; BREAD AND CHEESE, Dor, Som; FAIRY CHEESES, Som, Yks; FLIBBERTY GIBBET, Som; GOOD NIGHT AT NOON, Som; HORSE BUTTON, Donegal; MALLACE, Dev, Som, Hants; MAWS, Notts, N'thum, Scot; PANCAKE PLANT, Som, Lincs; RAGS AND TATTERS, Dor, Som; ROUND DOCK, Som. (Somerset alone has something like twenty different names for this plant.)

Widespread and abundant on banks, roadsides and waste places, especially near the sea. Rather less common in Scotland. Flowers from June to October, five-petalled, purplish blossoms up to one inch across. The plant is coarse, bushy and often straggly, and carries crinkly, ivy-shaped leaves which are slightly clammy to touch when young.

Mallow blooms late into the autumn, and its flowers have a strange, artificial elegance that is unexpected in such an obviously hardy wayside weed. The mauve petals are arched like some porcelain decoration, and veined with deep purple streaks.

The leaves stay green and fresh almost all the year, but are best picked in the summer months, when they are pale and stretch like films of gelatine. Always wash your leaves well and discard any that have developed a brownish rust, or are embedded with tiny black insect eggs.

Mallow leaves can be cooked as a spinach, but they are extremely glutinous, and a more attractive way of using them is to make them into soup. In Arab countries the leaves of an almost identical species are the basis of the famous soup, melokhia:

94

Melokhia is one of Egypt's national dishes. It is an ancient peasant soup, the making of which is believed to be portrayed in pharaonic tomb paintings. The medieval melokhia seems to have been a little richer, incorporating fried minced meat and chicken balls. Today, only a few families add these. . . . Peasant women prepare this soup almost daily. Protein stock is too expensive, so they cook the leaves in water in which a few vegetables have been boiled. The leaves give the soup a glutinous texture. The women cook the soup in large pots, which they carry to the fields on their heads for the men to eat at midday. When the work is done and the men come home, they eat it again at dusk with equal pleasure. Melokhia has recently acquired a symbolic and patriotic importance in Egypt, for it represents the national, popular taste as opposed to the more snobbish and cosmopolitan taste of the old regime. Most families have their own special way of preparing it, and the proportions vary according to the financial means, position and preferences of the people who make it.

from Middle Eastern Food, by Claudia Roden

To make a fairly authentic version of melokhia in this country, take about a pound of young mallow leaves, cut off the stalks, wash well, and chop very small or purée in a blender. Boil in about two pints of chicken stock for ten minutes. Then prepare a garlic sauce by frying two crushed cloves of garlic in a little oil until golden brown, adding a dessert-spoonful of ground coriander, a pinch of cayenne pepper, and some salt, and mixing to a paste in the hot pan. Add this paste to the soup, cover the saucepan tightly and simmer for two or three minutes, stirring occasionally to prevent the leaves falling to the bottom.

The melokhia can then be served on its own, or with boiled rice, or pieces of cooked meat and vegetables.

Common mallow is also known for its small, round seeds, called 'cheeses' (from their shape, rather than their taste, which is mildly nutty). Children in country districts still pick and eat these, though they're such a diminutive mouthful that their taste and texture are barely noticeable.

Ground elder *Aegopodium podagraria* [A]   Pl. 4

Local names: GOUTWEED, HERB GERARD. ASHWEED, Som; BISHOP'S ELDER, IoW; DOG ELDER, Ches; DUTCH ELDER, Wilts; DWARF ELDER, Hants, IoW; FARMER'S PLAGUE,

N. Ire; GOAT'S FOOT, Dev; GROUND ASH, Corn, Som, War, Ches, Lincs; JACK-JUMP-ABOUT, Oxf, Herts, N'thants, War, Worc; KESH, Cumb; POTASH, Dev; WHITE ASH, Som; WILD ELDER, Bucks; Lincs; WILD ASH, Cumb.

Widespread and common in shady places under hedges, in gardens, etc. Occurs throughout the British Isles. Flowers June to August, white umbels on a creeping, hairless stem, never much more than 1′ to 2′ high. Leaves: finely toothed, in groups of three at the end of the leaf stems.

Neither an ash nor an elder, goutweed's leaves do bear a superficial resemblance to those of both these trees. It can often be found in quite large patches by roadsides and under garden hedges, its pale green leaves making a bright carpet in the shady places. Its continued presence in both habitats is a telling example of the persistence of some weeds in places where they were once cultivated and valued.

Ground elder was probably introduced to this country by the Romans. In the Middle Ages it was grown in gardens as a vegetable, and at roadside inns and monasteries as a quick palliative for travellers' gout. Advances in medical understanding put paid to the second of these functions and the growing preference for bland-tasting vegetables to the first. Any popularity it still retained was finally undermined by the imperialistic tendencies of its rootstock, which would quickly take over its host's garden. Even in the sixteenth century, when the plant was still being used as a pot-herb, John Gerard wrote complainingly of it:

Herbe Gerard [named not after the botanist, but after St Gerard, the patron of the gouty] groweth of it selfe in gardens, without setting or sowing and it is so fruitfull in his increase that where it hath once taken roote, it will hardly be gotten out again, spoiling and getting every yeere more ground, to the annoying of better herbes.

Still, it is an agreeable vegetable cooked like spinach, with an unusual, tangy flavour.

Bistort *Polygonum bistorta* [A] **Pl. 2**

Local names: ADDERWORT, Som; EASTER GIANT, Cumb:
EASTER LEDGES,Yks, West, Cumb: GENTLE DOCK, Notts;
GOOSE-GRASS, Som; MEEKS, Notts, PASSION DOCK, Derb,
Yks, N. Eng; PENCUIR KALE, Ayr; POOR MAN'S CABBAGE
Lancs; RED LEGS, War, Shrop; SNAKEWEED, Som, Hants,
Ches, Lanark, Banff.

Widespread and locally common in wet, hilly pastures throughout
the British Isles, except the South. Flowers June to August,
pink spikes topping off a straight, hairless stem about 2' high.
Leaves: triangular or arrow-shaped on long stalks.

In the early spring of 1971 the following advertisement appeared
in the Personal Column of *The Times*: 'Polygonum bistorta –
How is your Dock Pudding?' The copy invited entrants for
the first World Championship Dock Pudding Contest, to be held
in the Calder Valley in Yorkshire. Evidently the tradition of
eating bistort is far from dead in the north, for there were over
fifty competitors from this one valley alone.

Bistort is a plant of damp upland meadows, out of the range
of nibbling sheep (though one Calder Valley man claimed that
the best plants grew on his grandad's grave on Sowerby Top).
It usually appears as the basic ingredient of Easter Ledger, or
Easter Herb, Pudding. The bulk of the popular local names refer
to the plant's function in this pudding, from Passion Dock (from
Passion-tide, the last two weeks of Lent, which was the proper
time for eating this rather scant dish) to Easter Giant, a contraction of Easter Mangiant, (from the French *manger*, to eat).

There is an enormous variety of different recipes for the
Ledger Pudding, most of them originating in the Lake District.
This one is from Westmorland:

Take a good bagful of spring leaves, mainly bisort, but also young
nettle tops, dandelion leaves, lady's mantle, etc. Wash them well
and put into a little boiling water for ten minutes. Strain and
chop the leaves. Add one beaten egg, one hard-boiled egg chopped
small, butter, salt and pepper, and mix well into the leaves. Put
back in the saucepan, heat through, and then transfer to a hot
pudding basin to shape. The pudding was usually eaten with veal.

Two other leaves, rather indifferent eating by themselves, were often used in the Easter Herb Pudding mixture.

Lady's mantle *Alchemilla vulgaris* [B]

Widespread and common in grassy places, but rare in the South and East of England. Flowers May to September.

Red leg *Polygonum persicaria* [B]

Widespread and common throughout the British Isles in damp, shady places, near ditches, etc. Flowers June to October.

Common sorrel *Rumex acetosa* [A]   **Pl. 4**

Local names: BREAD AND CHEESE, Dev; BROWN SUGAR, Som; CUCKOO'S MEAT, Ches; DONKEY'S OATS, Dev; GIPSY'S BACCY, Som; GREEN SAUCE, Corn, Dev, Glos, War, Ches, Derb, Leic, Notts, Lincs, Lancs, Yks; RED SOUR LEEK, N. Ire; SALLETT, Bucks; SOLDIERS, Som; SORROW, Glos, IoW; SOUR DOCK, Dev, Dor, Som, Shrop, Ches, Lancs, Yks, Cumb; SOUR SODGE, Bucks; TOM THUMB'S THOUSAND FINGERS, Kent.

Widespread and common in grassland and heathy places, especially on acid soils, throughout the British Isles. Flowers May to August, spikes of small red and green flowers on a smooth stem 6″ to 2′ high. Leaves arrow-shaped and clasping the stem near the top of the plant.

Sorrel is one of the very first green plants to appear in the spring. The leaves can often be picked as early as February when other green stuffs are scarce. They are marvellously cool and sharp when raw, like young plum skins, but perhaps too acid for some palates, though John Clare has his parched fieldworkers in *The Shepherd's Calendar* chewing them neat:

> The mower gladly chews it down
> And slakes his thirst the best he may

For ways of preparing and cooking the acid leaves we must look not only to Tudor England but to contemporary France, where sorrel is a prized vegetable.

In Gerard's time, the leaves were boiled and eaten, or made into a green sauce for fish. For this they were pulped raw and mixed with sugar and vinegar. Dorothy Hartley describes a late seventeenth century recipe for the sauce, in which bread, apple, sugar and vinegar are boiled together until soft, them mixed, still hot, with sorrel purée. The mixture is then strained, yielding a thick green juice with a strong pungent taste.

Compare this earthy method with the more sophisticated French variety. Finely chop a handful of sorrel leaves, and cook till puréed in $\frac{1}{2}$ oz of butter. Stir in, very slowly, $\frac{1}{4}$ pint of cream which has been previously boiled (to avoid curdling with the acid from the sorrel). Then thin to taste with stock from the dish the sauce is to accompany. The variations between the two approaches are minor, to be sure, but say a great deal about the differences between the two national cuisines.

In France sorrel is used in an enormous variety of dishes. The chopped leaves are added to give a sharp flavour to the heavy soups of potato, lentil and haricot bean. The cooked puree is added to omelettes, or, like the sauce, served as an accompaniment to veal or fish dishes.

To make a sorrel soup, chop a pound of the leaves with a large onion and a sprig of rosemary. Mix well with one tablespoon of flour and simmer the mixture in 3 oz of butter for about ten minutes, stirring well all the time. Add two quarts of boiling water, two tablespoons of breadcrumbs and seasoning. Simmer for one hour. When ready, take off the boil and just before serving stir in a well-beaten mixture of two egg yolks and $\frac{1}{4}$ pint of cream.

The leaves of sorrel are also interesting as a vegetable in their own right. They are cooked like spinach, but soften and purée much quicker. Nor do they taste much like spinach, as some writers have suggested, but more like a vegetable rhubarb.

99

Stinging nettle *Urtica dioica*   [A]   **Pl. 4**

Local names: DEVIL'S LEAF, Som; HEG-BEG, Scot; HOKY-POKY, Dev.

Widespread and abundant in almost every sort of environment. Flowers June to September, thin catkins of tiny, undistinguished green flowers. A coarse, upright plant, growing up to four feet high, and covered with stinging hairs. Leaves toothed and heart-shaped.

Be warned; to be caught eating nettles will cause more consternation amongst your friends than the munching of any number of the more dubious entries in this book. They will never quite believe that the formic acid responsible for the sting is utterly destroyed by cooking, and that your stomach lining is not already being irrevocably corroded.

Yet the stinging nettle is probably the commonest of all edible wild plants, and one of the most useful. There is evidence that nettles were cultivated in eighteenth century Scandinavia, the coarse fibres of the stalks being used for cloth as well as the leaves for food. Samuel Pepys enjoyed a nettle 'porridge' on February 25, 1661, though he gives no details of the dish. Scott has the old gardener in *Rob Roy* raising nettles under glass as 'early spring kail'. And in the Second World War hundreds of tons were gathered annually in Great Britain for the extraction of chlorophyll and of dyes for camouflage nets.

Nettles should not be picked for eating after the beginning of June. In high summer the leaves become coarse in texture, unpleasantly bitter in taste and decidedly laxative. The best time of all for them is when the young shoots are no more than a few inches high. Pick the whole of these shoots, or, if you are gathering later in the year, just the tops and the young pale green leaves. It is as well to use gloves whilst doing this, even if you do have a Spartan belief in the protection of the firm grasp.

Before cooking your nettles remove the tougher stems and wash well. They can be used in a number of ways. As a straight vegetable they should be boiled gently in a closed pan for about fifteen minutes, in no more water than adheres to the leaves after washing. Strain off the water well, add a large knob of butter and plenty of seasoning (and perhaps some chopped onion), and simmer for a further five minutes turning and mashing all the while. The resulting purée is interestingly fluffy in texture, but rather insipid to taste, and for my money nettles are better used as additions to other dishes than as vegetables in their own right.

Nettle soup is one such dish. Boil the nettles as above, and press through a hair sieve or reduce to a fine purée in a blender. Melt an ounce of butter in a pan and stir in an ounce of flour and salt and pepper. Remove from the stove and beat in a pint of hot milk gradually till the mixture is quite smooth. Boil up this sauce and simmer for five minutes, stirring all the time. Then pour onto the nettle purée and mix thoroughly. Prepare some fried bread in bacon fat, and add to the soup before serving.

Another splendid recipe is for nettle haggis. The nettle purée is mixed with leeks and cabbage, freshly fried bacon and partially cooked oatmeal (or rice or barley), and the whole boiled for an hour or so in a muslin bag, and served with gravy.

Young nettle leaves have also been made into beer and used as the basis for a herbal tea.

Common comfrey *Symphytum officinale* [A]

Local names: ABRAHAM, ISAAC AND JOSEPH, Lincs; CHURCH BELLS, Som; COFFEE FLOWER, Som; GOOSEBERRY-PIE, Dev, Dor, Wilts, Suff; PIGWEED, Wilts; SNAKE, Dor; SUCKERS, Som.

Widespread and common in ditches and by river banks throughout the British Isles. Flowers June to October, white, cream, mauve or pink bells in clusters. The plant is a bushy, hairy perennial, growing up to 3' high, with dark-green spear-shaped leaves.

Comfrey (from the Latin *confervere*, to grow together) was the medieval herbalists' favourite bone-setter. The root was lifted in the spring, grated up and used as plaster is today. In a short while the mash would set as solid as a hard wood. The whole plant was in fact one of those 'wonder herbs' that was used for every sort of knitting operation from drawing splinters to healing ruptures. (Though quite how the following recommendation from Gerard fits into this, it is difficult to see:

The slimie substance of the roote made in a posset of ale, and given to drinke against the paine in the backe, gotten by any violent motion, as 'wrestling, or over much use of women, doth in fower or five daies perfectly cure the same . . .)

Today comfrey is an increasingly common plant of damp places, especially by running water. In this sort of habitat its broad, spear-shaped leaves are unmistakeable, even when the plant is not in bloom. They are dull and hairy underneath, a fine, dark, almost glossy green above, and with slightly idented reticulations, as if the leaves had been pressed against a mould.

It is the leaves which are now used in cookery (though rather more solid evidence has been found for the root's reputed medicinal qualities than is the case with many traditional remedies). Don't worry about their furriness; this disappears completely during cooking. Nor is there much need to be particular about the age of the leaves you use, for in my experience the older ones (provided of course they have not started to wither) have more flavour than the younger. One way of using them is to boil them like spinach, with plenty of seasoning. There is no need to add butter, as the leaves themselves are fairly glutinous.

The best recipe for comfrey leaves is a Teutonic fritter called *schwarzwurz*. Leave the stalks on your comfrey leaves, wash well, and dip into a thin batter made from egg, flour and water. Then fry the battered leaf in deep fat for not more than two minutes. For a more succulent result I stick two or three similarly-sized leaves together before battering. The crisp golden batter contrasts delightfully with the mild, glutinous leaves.

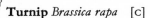

Turnip *Brassica rapa* [C]

The young leaves in spring can be boiled like spinach. (See ROOTS, p. 66).

Wild cabbage *Brassica oleracea* [c]

This scarce plant of the sea cliffs is probably the ancestor of all our garden cabbages. The various subspecies once grew widely round the shores of Western Europe and the Mediterranean, and it was probably one of the Southern varieties from which the domestic cabbage truly derives. Certainly the plant was under cultivation in Ancient Greece, and Pliny is careful to distinguish between wild and domesticated varieties. The Saxons and Celts cultivated them too, in Northern Europe. Since then centuries of breeding have turned the rough-shaped leaves of the wild plant into broccoli, brussels sprouts, cauliflower and kale.

Today the plant is rare in its natural habitat. Yet escaped garden *Brassicas* sometimes revert to this form if they are allowed to go to seed, the result no doubt of natural cross-pollination bringing the suppressed, wild characteristics back into dominance. You can tell them easily from the mustards and other related plants by their thick, greyish, fleshy leaves. They are bitter raw, but after a couple of good boilings and water changes, are quite acceptable to eat.

Charlock *Sinapis arvensis* [c]

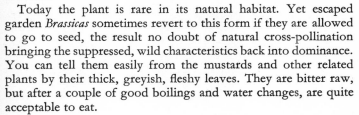

Geoffrey Grigson once rather unkindly called charlock 'a vegetable rat' because of its exceptional persistence as a weed of cultivated ground. The seeds can apparently remain fertile under grass for up to fifty years, and will spring into life again as soon as the ground is ploughed. Yet pest though it may be to the arable farmer, charlock's brilliant yellow flowers are not altogether unattractive.

Its leaves have served an honourable economic function, too. In spite of their bitterness, they were sold as a spinach in Dublin in the eighteenth century, and used still later, especially in times of hardship, on the island outposts of Great Britain.

Even rodents are not totally without their uses.

Spring beauty *Claytonia perfoliata* [c]

The leaves have been eaten as spinach, or raw in salads. See ROOTS, p. 66.

Pigweed *Amaranthus retroflexus* [C]

A curious casual of waste and cultivated ground, with dense spikes of dry, greenish flowers. The plant originated in tropical America and was much used by the Indians. The leaves, boiled, gave a particularly mild green vegetable, and the black seeds were ground into flour.

Jewel-weed *Impatiens capensis* [C]   **Pl. 4**

The jewel-weed or orange balsam is an increasingly frequent plant along the banks of rivers and canals in the South of England. If it is spared from British Waterway's herbicide sprays, it can often form magnificent bushes, up to 4′ high and festooned with mottled orange, nasturtium-like bells.

Jewel-weed is an introduction from North America and was not found in the wild in this country until 1822. It would be sad to start butchering such a new and handsome immigrant for food, but in its native land the young leaves and stems are used as a vegetable.

Monks rhubarb *Rumex alpinus* [C]

An uncommon species of dock, with large heart-shaped leaves. Monks rhubarb was introduced as a pot-herb in the Middle Ages, and in the parts of Scotland and the North of England where it still grows, it is rarely found far from houses.

Curled dock *Rumex crispus* [C]

The most widespread of all our docks, growing as happily in seaside shingle as in suburban field edges. The crinkly leaves, which can grow up to a foot long, are bitter, but have been used as a vegetable in the United States. The leaves are gathered very young and cooked with bacon or ham, and a little vinegar.

The leaves of our commonest dock, the broad-leaved dock (*Rumex obtusifolius*) have been used in the same way, though they are even more bitter.

Patience dock *Rumex patientia*   [C]   **Pl. 4**

A striking plant, which often grows more than 6′ in height, and
looks like a tall, rough rhubarb gone to seed. Like *Rumex alpinus*
it was introduced as a pot-herb, and can now only be found in
waste ground in the London area.

In America, where it is also an introduction, patience dock
is still cultivated in a few gardens.

Lungwort *Pulmonaria officinalis*   [C]   **Pl. 4**

A close relative of common comfrey, lungwort is a frequent
escape from gardens, where it used to be grown as a medicine
'against the infirmities and ulcers of the lungs'. Gerard also
recommends it as a boiled vegetable. It is an intriguing flower,
much like comfrey in its variably coloured flowers, but with its
leaves covered with a rash of white spots.

Oyster plant *Mertensia maritima*   [C]

Another relative of the comfrey. The oyster plant grows on a few
stretches of coastal shingle in Scotland, in prostrate mats. Its fleshy
leaves have been eaten both raw and cooked, and are said to taste
like oysters.

Ratstail plantain *Plantago major*   [C]

The ratstail, or great, plantain is one of those plants that
positively thrives on rough treatment. The more you walk
on it or mow it the better it thrives. The North American
Indians went as far as to call it 'English Man's Foot', for
wherever the white men walked and worked, plantain followed. Its rosettes of ribbed oval leaves are abundant on
lawns and footpaths.

The young leaves have been used as a salad herb, but I find
them too tough and bitter when raw, and would advise them to
be well cooked as a spinach.

Giant bellflower *Campanula latifolia*   [c]   **Pl. 4**

A magnificent flower of woods and hedgebanks in the northern
regions of the British Isles, up to five feet high with large, blue,
bell-like flowers. The young shoots have been eaten like spinach
in the past. To take them nowadays would be inexcusable.

Goosegrass *Galium aparine*   [c]

A great children's plant, which clings mercilessly to trousers
and coats and any rough surface which brushes against it. If you
look at a section of the stalk or leaf under a microscope you will
see that the plant's sticking power is due to the wicked hook-like
bristles which cover every part of it. Seen like this, they look
positively dangerous, and certainly not fit to eat. But look at
the hooks again after the plant has been plunged into boiling
water for a few seconds, and you will see that they have 'melted'
and quite lost their forbidding sharpness.

Boiled as a spinach before the hard round seeds appear, goose-
grass makes tolerable eating, and can, moreover, be picked
through snow and frost when few other green plants are to be
found. John Evelyn recommends the young shoots in spring
soups and puddings.

Few plants can have had their various parts put to so many
ingenious uses. The seeds have been roasted and used as a coffee.
In green state they were used to adorn the tops of lacemaker's
pins: the young seeds were pushed on to the pins to make a sort
of padded head. And some books report that the prickly stems
and leaves were used to strain hair out of fresh milk.

Red valerian *Centranthus ruber*   [c]

In France and Italy the very young leaves of this plant are
sometimes boiled with butter as greens, or eaten raw in salads –
though they are rather bitter used this way.

Red valerian was introduced to Britain from Southern Europe
in the sixteenth century, and was a great favourite of Gerard's,
though he ascribed no practical uses for the plant. Its clusters
of red flowers now adorn many stony and rocky places in the
South-West.

Stems

Sea kale *Crambe maritima* [A]   **Pl. 5**

Widespread but extremely local on sand and shingle near the
sea. Flowers June to August. A cabbage-like plant, growing in
large clumps with huge grey-green leaves, very fleshy and glau-
cous. The flowers are white and four-petalled, and grow in a
broad cluster.

I found my first sea kale through a pair of binoculars, on a
barren stretch of North Norfolk shingle over fifty miles from
the nearest record in the *Atlas of the British Flora*. It was the only
plant in sight and was hunched over the sand like some heavy,
stranded crustacean. Some of the leaves were nearly two feet
long, and had the texture of rubber sheet. They looked amazingly
appetising, and I cut off a few for supper. They were so heavy
and unwieldy that I had to improvise a driftwood and twine
sling to get them the six miles home.

Now I must confess that all this was before I knew very much
about the sea kale. I had read that it was prized as a delicacy
and to me the fleshy green leaves seemed the most obvious part
to use. That evening we boiled and boiled them, for nearly an
hour and a half. They seemed quite immutable, changing colour
a little, but holding that massive texture to the end. Eventually
we ate them as they were. It was the most powerful and tangy
taste I have ever experienced, like chewing the remains of a
sunken battleship.

Later, of course, I learned that it was not the leaves that were
normally eaten, but the young, white stems. There is little
doubt that in coastal areas the use of this part of the plant as a
vegetable dates back centuries before it was taken into cultivation.
In many areas on the south coast villagers would watch for the
shoots to appear, pile sand and shingle round them to blanch
out the bitterness and cut them in the summer to take to the
markets in the nearest big town.

At this time sea kale was a relatively common plant around the coasts. But in 1799, the botanist William Curtis wrote a pamphlet called *Directions for the culture of the Crambe Maritima or Sea Kale, for the use of the Table.* As a result the vegetable was taken up by Covent Garden, and demand for the naturally growing shoots increased greatly. This intensive collection was to have the effect of substantially reducing the population of wild sea kale.

Now the vegetable is out of fashion, but the wild plant shows no signs of regaining its former status. So be sparing if you do pick it, and do not take more than two or three stems from each plant. Use the lower parts of the leaf stalks, particularly any that you can find which have been growing under the ground. (They sometimes push their way through up to 3′ of shingle.) You could even adopt a local plant, and blanch the stems like coastal dwellers used to. If you object to heaps of shingle on the beach, cover the growing shoots with seaweed. However you grow them, when harvesting you will need a sharp knife to cut through the thick stems.

To cook the sea kale, cut the stems into manageable lengths and boil in salted water until tender (about 20 minutes). Then serve and eat with melted butter, like asparagus. Alternatively, use lemon juice or Sauce Hollandaise.

Marsh samphire, Glasswort *Salicornia europaea* [A] Pl. 5

Local names: SAMPHIRE, E. Ang, Lincs, N. Eng; SEMPER, N'thum; SAMPION, Ches; PICKLE PLANT, Cumb.
Common and plentiful on saltmarshes round most British coasts. Flowers August to September. Glassworts are highly succulent plants and vary from single unbranched stems to thick stubbly bushes up to 1′ tall. The stems are plump, shiny and jointed. Flowers minute, and only really visible as one or two white to red stamens growing out of the junction in the stems.

I have always had a special affection for marsh samphire. It was the plant which first made me aware that there was rather more to edible wild plant use than picking blackberries and roasting chestnuts. But even in its own right samphire is a real character. It is still surrounded by a wealth of folklore about when and where it should be picked. The plant is ready for picking, so they say, on the longest day (and so it usually is), and the healthiest specimens are those that have been 'washed by every tide.'

Picking samphire brings out the absurd in all but the most reserved of souls. The plant has a liking for execrably muddy situations, and grows in such abundance on some saltmarshes that communal picking seems the natural way to cope with it: a combination of circumstances that hardly encourages a serious frame of mind. You go out at low tide, with buckets and wellingtons, through the sea-aster and wormwood in the rough ground at the edge of the saltings, on to the tidal reaches where the crop grows. This is a world criss-crossed by deep and hidden creeks, by which you will be tripped, cut off and plastered up to the thigh with glistening wet mud. In these creeks the samphire grows tall and bushy, like an amiable desert cactus. After the notorious 1953 floods in East Anglia, when all types of unconventional nutrients must have been washed into the marshes, a bush of samphire 6′ tall and as thick as a leek at the base was discovered in one Norfolk creek. It was carried away on a bicycle crossbar and later hung up above the bar of a local pub.

On the poorer, sandier flats the size of the plants is less distinctive and they tend to grow as single shoots not more than 6″ high. Yet they make up for this in sheer numbers. Often a bed can completely carpet several acres of marsh, and look as though it could be cut with a lawnmower.

When you have found your patch there is no way of escaping half an hour in a stooping position to do the picking. There are those who have tried to cut and lift the shoots with shears, but samphire is a wily and demanding plant, and cut like this will just flop over into the mud. Hunched up and grubbing about in the mud is the only way to appreciate the flavour of samphire-gathering. If at this stage you can't keep your adult composure then perhaps you should stick to frozen broccoli.

There are two ways of actually picking the plant. Early in the season, whilst the shoots are still thin and tender, they should be pinched off above the root. Later in the year, when most of the growth has finished and the plants have developed a tough fibrous core, the whole plant can be pulled up. There are slightly different ways of cooking the young shoots and the whole plant.

When you have got your samphire home, wash it well and remove the pieces of seaweed that will inevitably be stuck to some of the plants. But never leave samphire to stand in water for more than a few hours. In stagnant water it quickly begins to decay. If you wish to keep it for a few days before eating choose a dry place open to the air.

The very young shoots, picked in June or July, make a crisp and tangy salad vegetable. Try chewing some sprigs straight from the marsh. They are very refreshing in spite of their slightly salty taste. To cook them boil them in a little water for about ten minutes, drain and simmer with a knob of butter. They go very well with poultry and lamb.

The whole plants picked in August and September are best served as an asparagus-like starter. Leave the roots on and boil the plants upside down in a saucepan of water. Drain, and serve whole in a bowl, with molten butter. (Samphire plants, being rather low in weight, cool off quickly, so it is as well to melt the butter first before pouring it onto the vegetable.) Eat by holding the roots and sliding the stems between the teeth, to draw the flesh off the tough central spine.

Another way of using samphire is to pickle it. This was once done by filling jars with the chopped shoots, covering with spiced vinegar, and placing in a baker's oven as it cooled off over the weekend. I would imagine that the result of 48 hours' simmering would be on the sloppy side to say the least. To maintain the crisp texture of the plant and at least some of its brilliant green colour it is best to do no more than put it under cold pickling vinegar.

However it is used marsh samphire is a delectable plant, and there are signs that it is becoming more popular. It is appearing on an increasing number of East Anglian market stalls, and even – at vastly inflated prices – in some restaurants.

Alexanders *Smyrnium olustratum*   [A]   **Pl. 5**

Local names: ALICK, Kent; HELLROOT, Dor; MEGWEED, Suss; SKIT, Corn; WILD CELERY, IoW.

Widespread and locally abundant in hedgebanks and waste

places, especially near the sea. Flowers April to June, umbels of yellow-green flowers. A bushy, solid-stemmed hairless plant growing up to 4' high. Leaves glossy, toothed, on groups of three at the end of the leaf stalk; the other end being joined to the main stem by a substantial sheath.

The Romans brought alexanders to this country from the Mediterranean, as a pot-herb. It thrived, became naturalised, and was still being planted in kitchen gardens in the early eighteenth century.

Today it can often be found growing abundantly in hedge-banks near the coast. It sprouts early and rapidly in the spring, and its bright, glossy leaves can sometimes be seen pushing through the January snows.

Most parts of the plant have been used in the kitchen at one time or another. A seventeenth century botanist described a soup made of the upper part of the roots. The flower buds were used in medieval salads. And the young leaves make a spicy addition to modern green salads.

The most succulent part of the plant is the stem. You should cut those leaf stems which grow near the base of the plants, where they are thick and have been partially blanched by the surrounding grass or the plant's own foliage. You should be able to cut about six inches of pinkish stalk from each stem (discarding the greener bits). Don't be put off by the plant's rather cloying Angelica smell; this disappears almost completely with cooking.

Cook these stems in boiling water for not more than ten minutes. Then eat them like asparagus, with molten butter. They have a wonderfully delicate texture, and a pleasantly aromatic taste.

Rock samphire *Crithmum maritimum* [A]   Pl. 5

Local names: CAMPHIRE, Cumb; PASSPER, Scot; ROCK SEMPER, Yks, N'thum.

Frequent on rocky coasts in the south and west. Flowers July to September, yellow umbels. A squat, bushy plant growing up to one foot high. Stems are hairless and solid, and the leaves, fleshy, grey-green and cut into narrow untoothed leaflets.

This the plant whose precarious cliff-face gathering Shakespeare called a 'dreadful trade' in *King Lear*. Its name is confusing, for the plant bears no sort of relation to marsh samphire, *Salicornia europaea*. Even the habitats are different. Rock samphire has a preference for the side of cliffs, and it was from this habitat that it was often gathered along with gulls' eggs. From Dover and the Isle of Wight samphire was despatched in casks of brine to London, where in the nineteenth century wholesalers would pay up to four shillings a bushel for it.

Luckily there is no need to risk your life half-way down a rock face to find it. The plant also grows quite frequently in shingle, and you can often find it by its smell alone, warm but slightly sulphurous. Both stems and leaves are used, but before cooking remove any leaves that have begun to turn slimy, and any hard parts of the stalk. Then boil in water for about a quarter of an hour, and serve with melted butter. To eat it, suck the fleshy parts away from the stringy veins. In Yorkshire it was cooked in this way and then eaten cold with bread.

Rock samphire is probably best known as a pickle:

'Let it be gathered about Michaelmas or in the spring and put two or three hours into a brine of water and salt, then into a clean tinned brass pot with three parts of strong white wine vinegar and one part of water and salt or as much as will cover the sampier, keeping the vapour from issuing out by pushing down the pot lid, and so hang it over the fire for half an hour only. Being taken off let it remain cover'd till it be cold and then put it up into small barrels or jars with the liquor and some fresh vinegar, water and salt, and thus it will keep very green. If you be near the sea that water will supply the place of brine. This is the Dover Receit.'

From *Acetaria*, John Evelyn, 1699

Rock samphire was John Evelyn's favourite vegetable, and though his brass pot is probably safer replaced by some earthenware dish, the recipe can be followed exactly.

The most curious recipe I have come across for this vegetable dates from the mid-seventeenth century, and is for a samphire hash. Take about a quarter of a pound of chopped samphire and mix with a handful of diced pickled cucumbers and some capers. Boil in a pint of stock to which has been added two tablespoons of wine vinegar, the juice and grated peel of one lemon, pepper and nutmeg. Simmer for half an hour. Take off the boil and gradually add slivers of butter and the yolk of an egg, stirring continuously, until the mixture thickens.

This sauce was used as a garnish for meat, and the whole dish dressed with fresh samphire leaves and bright red barberries.

Burdock *Arctium minus* [A]   **Pl. 5**

Local names: BACHELOR'S BUTTONS, Dev, Som; BAZZIES, Kent; BUTTER-DOCK, Corn; CLEAVERS, Som; CLITE, Som, Glos; CLOUD-BURR, Yks, Cumb; CLOG-WEED, Wilts; COCKLES, Dor, Wilts, Hants; CUCKOLD BUTTONS, Som; DONKEYS, Som; EDDICK, Ches; FLAPPER-BAGS, Scot; GIPSY COMB, Berks, Notts; HURR-BURR, Som, Shrop, Leic; KISSES, Som; LOPPY MAJOR, Som; PIG'S RHUBARB, Dor; STICKY JACKS, Som; SWEETHEARTS, Dor; TOUCH-ME-NOT, Som; TUZZY-MUZZY, Dev, Som; WILD RHUBARB, Som.

Widespread and common throughout the British Isles, at the edges of woods, and on roadsides and waste ground. Flowers July to September. A stiff, bushy plant, up to 3' high, conspicuous early in the year for its large, floppy, heart-shaped leaves, and later for its stout branching stems. The flower-heads are egg-shaped and thistle-like, and turn at the fruiting stage into the well-known prickly burs.

Burdock is often mistaken for rhubarb, as many of its local names testify. Often there is nothing to be seen of the plant except its huge leaves draped over the ground. The parts to pick are the young leaf stems which begin to sprout round about May (after September they are too tough and stringy). The stems should be cut into 2" lengths and the hard outer peel stripped off. This will leave you with a moist core about the thickness of a pipe-cleaner. This can be chopped and used raw in salads, boiled and served with butter like asparagus, or added to meat soups as Gerard recommends.

It has an intriguing and elusive taste: crisp, nutty, with hints of fennel and of the skins of cucumbers.

In Japan the plant is cultivated, and in addition to the leaf and flower stalks, the tough black root is used, normally in a finely chopped form.

Reed *Phragmites communis*   [A]   **Pl. 5**

Widespread and often abundant by the edges of marshes, swamps,
and in shallow fresh, or brackish water. Flowers August onwards.
A tall grass, 5′ to 8′ high, often forming dense beds. The leaves
are flat, long and pointed. The flower heads are long, dense and
branched, with numerous plumy purple spikes. In the autumn
these fade to a pale brown, and the stems become hard canes.

This is the common reed which so readily forms dense beds in
still, shallow water. It is something of a cheat on my part to
include it in this section, since the stems are not eaten in any
of the ways described in the previous pages. But they have
been used in some fascinating ways that I felt were worth men-
tioning here.

When the stalks are still green it often happens that they are
punctured or broken in some way. When this happens a sugary
substance slowly exudes and hardens into a gum. The North
American Indians used to collect this and break it into balls which
they ate as sweets. Another Indian way of preparing a sweet from
the plant was to cut the reeds when still green, dry them, grind
them and sift out the flour. This contains so much sugar that
when it is placed near a fire it swells, browns, and is eaten like
toasted marshmallow.

Marsh thistle *Cirsium palustre*   [C]

A tall, common thistle of grassy places and woods, especially
on wet ground. The young shoots have been used like burdock
in some European countries. The prickles and the tough outer
peel are removed, and the stalks then used in salads or boiled.

Russian thistle *Salsola pestifera*   [C]

A rare but increasing casual in the British Isles. In some of the
western states of America, where the plant is plentiful, the plants
are cut when a few inches high, trimmed of their worst thorns,
boiled and served with a cream sauce on toast.

Milk thistle *Silybum marianum*   [C]   **Pl. 5**

Centuries ago this handsome thistle was introduced into Western
European gardens from the Mediterranean, for use as a pot-herb.
It is a distinctive plant, growing up to 6′ high, and its spiny
leaves are intricately veined in white. Almost all parts of the plant
were eaten. The leaves were trimmed of prickles and boiled.
The stems were peeled, soaked in water to remove the bitterness
and then stewed like rhubarb. Even the spiny bracts that surround
the broad flowerhead were eaten like globe artichokes.

Milk thistle is widespread but only locally common in the
British Isles. It is liable to spring up in any waste place, but
prefers areas near the sea, and especially the Thames Estuary.

Asparagus *Asparagus officinalis*   [C]   **Pl. 5**

There are two varieties of asparagus growing wild in this country.
Asparagus officinalis subsp. *prostratus*, the prostrate, native sub-
species, and subsp. *officinalis*, the introduced garden variety which
is now naturalised in the wild in a few places. Neither type grows
as sumptuously as cultivated specimens, and both are uncommon.
So picking is not really to be recommended.

The part of both plants which is eaten is the fat shoot, or
'spear', which grows from the rootstock in early summer. Later
this matures into a ferny leaf structure, tiny yellowish bell-like
flowers and orange berries.

Butcher's broom *Ruscus aculeatus*   [C]

A close relative of asparagus, which grows locally as a stiff
evergreen bush in dry woodlands in the south of England.
The young shoots have been eaten in some areas of Europe.

Bath asparagus, Spiked star of Bethlehem
Ornithogalum pyrenaicum   [C]   **Pl. 5**

It would be criminal casually to pick this exquisite lily, which
grows in no more than half a dozen English counties. Yet
while the flowers are still in bud in May, bunches of the plant
are picked around Bristol and Bath, and sold to be eaten like
asparagus.

Seaweeds

Although they reproduce by spores, not flowers, seaweeds have seasons of growth like other plants. They produce shoots in the spring, grow quickly and luxuriantly during the summer, and wither in the winter. The best months to gather most seaweeds are May and June.

Seaweeds obtain their food entirely from the surrounding sea water and do not have roots in the conventional sense. However they do have hold-fasts, by which they attach themselves to rocks and stones, and from which the stem-like part, or stipe, grows. The weed itself can regenerate from a cut stipe, provided the cut is not too near the hold-fast. So if you are cutting seaweed rather than gathering leaves which have been washed free of their moorings, leave plenty of stipe so that the weed can grow again.

Before cooking any seaweed always wash thoroughly in fresh water to remove sand, shells and other shoreline debris which may have stuck to it.

Seaweeds are rich in minerals, particularly iodides, and you may take a little while to get used to their flavours. But do give them a fair chance; they are intriguing foods, and quite undeserving of their freakish, joke-book reputation.

Carragheen, Irish moss *Chondrus crispus* [A]   **Pl. 5**

Widespread on stones and rocks on temperate Atlantic shores. Grows in clusters of purple-brown fronds. These have a distinctly flat stalk, and branch repeatedly into a rough fan shape.

Carragheen is an important source of alginates – vegetable gelatines – which are used for thickening soups, emulsifying ice-creams and setting jellies. They can also be made into thin, durable films for use as edible sausage skins.

You can find carragheen on almost any Western or Southern shore. It is best gathered young, in April or May, and either used immediately or carefully dried. To use the weed fresh, wash it well, add one cup of weed to three cups of milk or water and sugar and flavouring to taste. Then simmer slowly until most of the weed has dissolved. Remove any undissolved fragments and pour into a mould to set. This produces a basic Irish moss blanc-mange or jelly, depending on whether you use milk or water. Ginger is good as a flavouring, and can be added in the form of the chopped root during the simmering of the weed.

To dry the weed, wash it well, and then lay out to dry on a wind-free surface out-of-doors. Wash it from time to time with fresh water, or simply leave it in the rain. After a while it will become bleached to a creamy-white colour. Trim off any tough stalks, dry thoroughly indoors, and then store in bags. The dried weed can be used exactly as if it were fresh.

Carragheen grows abundantly in the Channel Islands and during the war it was gathered and sold in shops. The demand was so great that boats had to be used in spite of the large number of mines in the area. The weed was used to thicken soups and stews.

Two other commonly occurring weeds can be used to provide jelly bases, like carragheen.

Gigartina stellata [B]

Common and often abundant on the middle and lower shore, especially on the West coast.

Kelp *Laminaria digitata* [B]

Grows at the low-water mark on rocky shores all round the coast. As well as a salad vegetable, is used as a source of alginates.

Laver *Porphyra umbilicalis* [A] **Pl. 5**

Common all round Britain, especially on exposed shores on the West coast. Grows on rock and stones at most levels of the beach, especially where the stones are likely to be covered with sand. The fronds are thin, irregularly-shaped purple membranes.

In the south-west of Wales laver is considered a great delicacy, and it sells briskly in many food shops to those who don't want the bother of gathering it for themselves.

Yet it is one of the easier seaweeds to find and recognise, its translucent purple fronds liable to crop up on almost all levels of the shore. In Japan it is cultivated. Bundles of bamboo are placed on the sea bottom, just offshore, and transferred to fresh river water once the weed has established itself. In these conditions the laver apparently grows softer and more extensive fronds. The Chinese and Japanese make very varied use of their laver, in soups and stews, as a covering round rice balls, and in pickles and preserves.

In Britain there have been two classic, traditional uses: laver sauce for mutton, and laverbread. The first stage in any laver recipe is to reduce the weed to a sort of rough purée. First wash it well and then simmer in a little water until it is like well-cooked spinach. This is best done in a double saucepan as the laver sticks easily. This mush, if transferred to a jar, will keep well for several days.

It is this purée which is sold in Wales under the name of laverbread. It ends up in the place you would least expect it, on the breakfast table, rolled in oatmeal and fried in bacon fat.

To make laver sauce, beat up two cupfuls of the purée with an oz of butter and the juice of one Seville orange.

A number of seaweeds can be cooked like laver and used as a vegetable.

Sea lettuce *Ulva lactuca*   [B]

Quite common on all types of shore, attached to stones and rocks, sea lettuce is especially fond of places where water runs into the sea.

Monostroma grevillei   [B]

Very similar to sea lettuce, though less common, and more delicate in texture.

Dulse *Rhodymenia palmata* [B]

Abundant on stones on the middle and lower shores.

Dulse has been eaten raw as a salad, and in New England the dried fronds are used as a relish. It is a very tough weed, and as a cooked vegetable needs up to five hours simmering.

Laminaria saccharina [B]

Often found attached to small stones on muddy and sandy flats.

The young stipes of this weed used to be sold in Scotland under the name of 'tangle'. One writer describes their taste as resembling that of peanuts.

A composite jelly, made from this weed and dulse and called *Pain des Algues*, used to be prepared on the coast of Armorica.

Alaria esculenta [B]

Commonest on exposed shores, where it takes the place of *Laminaria digitata*.

Enteromorpha intestinalis [B]

Abundant on salt marshes and in dikes and rocky pools. A weed which should be picked in the early spring.

Bladder wrack *Fucus vesiculosus* [B]

Abundant on the middle shore.

Pepper dulse *Laurencia pinnatifida* [B]

An infrequent weed which forms dense tufts in rock crevices on the middle shore. Pepper dulse is very pungent and is usually used as a condiment. In Iceland it has been employed as a substitute for chewing tobacco.

Iridaea edulis [B]

Has been eaten both raw, and after being pinched between two hot irons.

The remaining three entries in this section are not seaweeds, but being non-flowering plants fit more satisfactorily into this section than anywhere else.

Maidenhair fern *Adiantum capillis-veneris* [C]

A rare and delicate fern which grows on sheltered limestone cliffs in a few localities in the West. In the eighteenth and nine-teenth centuries it was used as a garnish to sweet dishes. Later it formed the basis of *capillaire* which was a popular flavouring at the turn of the century. The fern (imported from Iceland) was simmered in water for several hours, and the liquid made into a thick syrup with sugar and orange-water. *Capillaire* was mixed with fruit juice and water to form soft drinks.

Iceland moss *Cetraria islandica* [C]

This rust-brown lichen grows amongst the heather and other ground plants on moorlands in Scotland and the North of England. An edible jelly is sometimes made by boiling the plant, which is first soaked in water to remove the bitter flavour.

Rock tripe *Umblicaria pustulata* [C]

This is a strange lichen, growing like a mat of pebbles on rocks and walls in Western regions of Britain. It is edible if cooked like a seaweed, and some Arctic explorers have survived off it for weeks on end. Yet they have more praise for its powers of nourishment than for its taste; one gives the rather forbidding description 'a little like tapioca with a slight flavouring of liquorice'.

Herbs

'To proceed then to this knowledge of cookery, you shall understand, that the first step thereunto is to have knowledge of all sorts of herbs belonging to the kitchen, whether they be for the pot, for salletts, for sauces for servings, or for any other seasoning or adorning: which skill of knowledge of the herbs, she must get by her own true labour experience, and not by my relation, which would be much too tedious; and for the use of them, she shall see it in the composition of dishes and meats hereafter following. She shall also know the time of the year, month, and Moon, in which all herbs are to be sown; and when they are in their best flourishing, that gathering all herbs in their height of goodness, she may have the prime use of the same.'

The English Hus-Wife, Gervase Markham, 1653

Sane, practical words, particularly at a time when the doctrine of signatures was still widely fashionable. This decreed that the medicinal qualities of a plant and the disorders it was destined to heal, could be divined by the 'signature' on the plant, that is the organ or illness which was suggested by the shape, colour or smell of a particular part. So the round, patchy leaves of lungwort were prescribed for diseases of the chest, and henbane seeds given for toothache because of a presumed similarity between the shape of the husk and a molar. Not all the remedies were so ingenious or the associations as pleasing to the imagination as this, and most were even more wildly off the mark therapeutically than those arrived at by astrology. This too was influential at the time, and was another activity which had to suffer John Evelyn's level-headed scrutiny:

Let none then consult Culpeper, or the Figure-flingers, to inform them when the governing Planet is in its Exaltation; but look upon the Plants themselves, and judge of their Vertues by their own complexion.

Acetaria

I mention all this because the history of folk medicine has somewhat clouded the meaning of the word 'herb'. For this section I shall use the meaning as it is understood in modern kitchens; that is a leaf plant which is used not as a food in its own right, but as a source of flavouring for other foods. Admittedly certain of the species I have included here do have *bona fide* medicinal pedigrees, and others can be used as *pot*-herbs by themselves. But it is because of their value as flavourings that they have been chosen.

Here we come up immediately against a curious difference between herbs and the other wild vegetables I have discussed in this book. Whereas most wild foods are more strongly flavoured than their cultivated relatives, the reverse is true of herbs; being valued principally for their flavouring qualities, it is these which domestication has attempted to intensify, not delicacy, size, succulence or any of the other qualities that are sought after in staple vegetables. You will find, consequently, that with wild herbs you will need up to double the quantities you normally use of the cultivated variety.

A few words about the collection, storage and drying of herbs. The best time to pick a herb, especially for the purposes of drying, is just as it is coming into flower. This is the stage at which the plant's nutrients and aromatic oils are still mainly concentrated in the leaves, yet it will have a few blossoms to assist with the identification. Gather your herbs in dry weather and preferably early in the morning before they have been exposed to too much sun. Wet herbs will tend to develop mildew during drying, and specimens picked after long exposure to strong sunshine will inevitably have lost some of their natural oils by evaporation.

Cut whole stalks of the herb with a knife to avoid damaging the parent plant. If you are going to use the herbs fresh, strip the leaves and flowers off the stalks as soon as you get them home. If you are going to dry them, leave the stalks intact as you have picked them. To maintain their colour and flavour they must be dried as quickly as possible but without too intense a heat. They therefore need a combination of gentle warmth and good ventilation. A kitchen or well-ventilated airing cupboard is ideal. The stalks can be hung up in loose bunches, or spread thinly on a sheet of paper and placed on the rack above the stove. Ideally, they should also be covered by muslin, to keep out flies and insects and, in the case of hanging bundles, to catch any leaves that start to crumble and fall as they dry.

Drying normally takes about two to three weeks. During this period the stalks should be turned and rearranged regularly to make sure that all parts of the plant are equally exposed to air and warmth. Once the leaves are crisp they should be stripped from the stalks along with the flowers, and stored in clean, dry, airtight jars. When you are using dried herbs remember that contraction and loss of water during the drying process concentrates the flavour to about three times the strength of that in the fresh plant.

Meadowsweet *Filipendula ulmaria* [A]

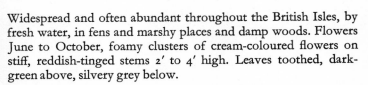

Local names: BITTERSWEET, Yks; COURTSHIP-AND-MATRI-MONY, Cumb; GOAT'S BEARD, Dor, Dev; HAYRIFF, Shrop; KISS-ME-QUICK, Som; MAID OF THE MEAD, Ches; MAY OF THE MEADOW, War; MEADOW-SOOT, Wilts; MEADWORT, Som; NEW MOWN HAY, Som; QUEEN OF THE MEADOW, Dev, Dor, Som, War, Lincs, Yks, N'thum, N. Eng, Scot, N. Ire, Ork; QUEEN'S FEATHER, Som; SUMMER'S FAREWELL, Dev, Dor; SWEET HAY, Dor, Suss; TEA FLOWER, Som; WIREWEED, Hants.

Widespread and often abundant throughout the British Isles, by fresh water, in fens and marshy places and damp woods. Flowers June to October, foamy clusters of cream-coloured flowers on stiff, reddish-tinged stems 2' to 4' high. Leaves toothed, dark-green above, silvery grey below.

One of the most summery of all our wild plants. In July the frothy flowerheads of meadowsweet can transform a heavy riverside meadow. As so often is the case, local names reveal a great deal about the flower's characteristics and uses. Courtship-and-Matrimony refers to the difference in scent before and after crushing the plant. So, the fresh flowers are warm and heady, the crushed leaves more clinically sharp. When dried, both parts of the plant smell of new-mown hay (hence the names Sweet Hay, Hayriff). It was these dried leaves that were used to give an especially aromatic bouquet to port, claret and mead, and it is to this function that the name Meadwort refers, not its preference for growing in meadows.

The leaves can be used for flavouring almost any sort of drink. and can double for woodruff (p. 137) if that plant is unobtainable.

Cow parsley *Anthriscus sylvestris* [A]

Local names: numerous, including – ADDER'S MEAT, Som; BAD MAN'S OATMEAL, Yks; DEVIL'S PARSLEY, Ches; COW CHERVIL, Som; ELD-ROT, Dor; GIPSY LACES, Dor, Som; KELK, Wilts, Suss, Kent, Surr, Yks, Dur, N'thum; LADY'S NEEDLEWORK, Glos; MAYWEED, Worc; MOONLIGHT, Wilts; RABBIT'S MEAT, Dev, Som, Suss, War, Lincs, Yks; SCAB FLOWER, Cumb; WILD PARSLEY, Lincs, Rad.

Widespread and abundant on footpaths, roadsides, banks etc. Flowers April to June, umbels of tiny white flowers. The plant is 2' to 4' high, with hollow, green, furrowed stems, hairy near the bottom of the plant but smooth above. The leaves are grass-green, slightly downy, and much divided, looking very like wedge-shaped ferns.

No plant shapes our roadside landscape more than cow parsley. In May its lacy white flowers teem along every path and hedge-bank. It grows prolifically; road verges can be blanketed with it for miles on end, and be broadened several feet by its overhanging foliage.

This provident plant has been almost totally overlooked as a herb, even though one of its less common botanical names is wild chervil. It is in fact the closest wild relative of cultivated chervil, *Anthriscus cerefolium*, a little coarser than that garden variety, maybe, but sharing the same fresh, spicy flavour.

Cow parsley is the first common umbelliferate to come into flower in the spring, and this is often enough to identify it positively. But since there are a number of related species which resemble it, and which can cause serious poisoning, I have included below some notes on the characteristics which un-equivocally identify cow parsley. The most dangerous sources of confusion are fool's parsley and hemlock, and it is with these plants in mind that I have selected the criteria. But I must stress that these few pointers are in no way a substitute for a well-illustrated field guide: they are merely intended to bring out the most prominent and useful differentiating characteristics.

Size: Fool's parsley rarely grows more than a foot high, and is a flimsy-looking, insubstantial plant, usually growing as separate individuals. Cow parsley grows up to 4' high, often in bushy clumps. Hemlock is an altogether more substantial plant, growing like a shrub up to 7'.

Stem: Fool's parsley has thin, hairless, ribbed and hollow stems. Cow parsley – stouter, paler green, furrowed and slightly hairy. Hemlock – very stout, smooth and purple-spotted.

In addition hemlock has an offensive, mousey smell when any part of it is bruised, and fool's parsley has unmistakeable drooping green bracts growing beneath the flowers, giving them a rather bearded appearance.

You should pick wild chervil as soon as the stems are sufficiently developed for you to identify it. Later in the year it becomes rather bitter. It dries well, so pick enough to last you through the off-season as well as for your immediate needs. But do not gather the plant from the sides of major roads; even if it has been spared the Highway Department's herbicides, it will certainly have been contaminated by car exhausts.

Chervil is a very versatile herb and small quantities make a lively addition to most sorts of salads, particularly cold potato, tomato, and cucumber. It also makes a good flavouring for hot haricot beans, and herb omelettes.

A second crop of non-flowering leaves often appears in the autumn and remains green throughout the winter, and those experienced enough to tell the plant from its leaves alone could do worse than pick some fresh for winter soups and casseroles. It goes well with hot baked potatoes, and as an addition to the French country dish cassoulet.

Wild celery *Apium graveolens* [A]   Pl. 6

Local names: SMALLAGE

Widespread but local in damp places near the sea, and mainly in the south and east of England. Flowers June to September. A strongly-smelling plant, growing about 1' to 2' high, with shiny, yellow-green leaves, shaped much like those of garden celery, and rather sparse white umbels of flowers.

Wild celery has suffered much abuse at the hands of writers on herbs – mainly, I suspect, by people who have never got beyond the rather overpowering smell to the stage of actually eating it. Some have gone as far as to say that it is unpalatable and even poisonous. It is categorically not the latter, and in my experience anything but the former.

Our early ancestors were less particular, and wild celery was certainly used quite extensively in medieval kitchens. The cultivated variety was developed comparatively late, probably in France and Italy, and was only introduced into this country in the 17th century. Domestication appears to have been aimed chiefly at softening the pungent odour of the plant, and fattening out the stem. There is no doubt that the smell is rather strong: the first time I came across the plant, growing abundantly at the edges of a road through a dense reed bed, it was like strolling through a village vegetable show on a hot afternoon. But much of this smell disappears on drying, leaving a herb which is exactly like strong celery in flavour, and ideal for soups. To make a straight cream of wild celery much richer and tangier than garden celery soup, pick a small bunch of the leaves, dry for about three weeks (in a little used room!) then simmer for about half an hour in some chicken stock. Strain, stir in a cupful of hot milk and serve immediately.

But even in the fresh, undried state, the taste is nothing like as powerful as might be expected. The stems are not of course as bity as those of the garden variety, but I have found that a few of them, chopped, make a brisk ingredient for salads.

Fennel *Foeniculum vulgare* [A]

Local names: FINKLE, Kent, Lincs, Yks, N. England, Scot; SPIGNEL, Som.

Locally distributed throughout the south of England, Midlands, East Anglia and Wales. Less common in the north and Scotland. Occurs on cliffs, waste ground and damp places, especially near the sea. Flowers early June to October; clusters of mustard yellow blossoms; leaves threadlike and aromatic. Height up to 5'.

There is apparently an old Welsh saying that : 'He who sees fennel and gather it not, is not a man, but a devil'. I doubt if one would want to encourage quite such an obsessive response, or the poor herb would be wiped out in a season. But see fennel's feathery sprays along the damp coast roadsides in early July, and you will understand the attraction it held for the early herbalists.

Its umbels of yellow flowers and smooth, threadlike leaves are elegantly soft, giving the plant a curiously foppish air beside the hairy yokels it shares living space with. Crush the leaves in your hand and they give off a powerful aromatic odour, reminiscent of aniseed. On a hot summer's day this is enough to betray the plant's presence, for the cool tang stands out from the heavy, sweet musks of hogweed and elder like a throwback to a sharp April morning.

Fennel occurs throughout the southern half of the British Isles, on cliffs as much as in dank meadows, but it tends to grow in rather localised patches. All parts of the plant are edible, from the stalks – if your teeth are strong enough – to the rather sparse bulb. (The larger fennel bulbs obtainable from some greengrocers belong to cultivated Florence fennel, *Foeniculum vulgare dulce*.) They all have a fresh, nutty flavour. But it is the thinner stalks, leaf sprays and seeds that are the most useful.

The green parts of the plant should be cut with a sharp knife as early in the summer as possible, and some (stalks included) hung up to dry for the winter. Fennel smells stronger as it dries, and after a few weeks a good-sized bunch will be powerful enough to scent a whole room. The seeds should be gathered late in October, just before they are fully dry.

Fennel was one of the Anglo-Saxon herbalists' nine sacred herbs, and later writers credit it with astonishingly versatile powers:

> In Fennel-seed, this vertue you shall find,
> Foorth of your lower parts to drive the winde.
> Of Fennel vertues foure they do recite,
> First it hath power some poysons to expell,
> Next, burning Agues will it put to flight,
> The stomack it doth cleanse, and comfort well:
> And fourthly, it doth keepe, and cleanse the sight,
> And thus the seede and herbe doth both excell.
>
> *The Englishman's Doctor*, 1608

Although fennel seeds are still mentioned in the British Pharmaceutical Codex as a remedy for 'winde' (no doubt the reason they are chewed after Indian meals) a more reliable range of uses today is as flavouring for fish dishes. Fennel is especially good with oily fish, though the tradition of using it in this way probably derives from nothing more than the plant's preference for coastal areas. The dried stalks form the basis of the famous Provençal red mullet dish, *rouget flambé au fenouil*. The finely chopped green leaves are also good to add to liver, potato salad, parsnips, and even, Len Deighton recommends, apple pie.

A dish that can really charm out and make use of the cool fragrance of fennel is okrochka, an exotic cold soup from Greece. It is a perfect dish on a warm evening, and utilises some of the other summer herbs you may gather in this section.

Mix two cartons of yoghourt (plain or apple) with roughly the same quantity of milk in a sizeable bowl. Add one cup of diced fresh cucumber, $\frac{1}{2}$ cup of chopped pickled cucumber or gherkin, $\frac{1}{2}$ cup of diced cooked chicken, and a handful of finely chopped fennel leaves. Add any other summer herbs that you have available – mint, parsley, and chives are particularly good – but they must be fresh, and not in such quantities that they mask the fennel. Season with salt and freshly ground pepper and put in the fridge for at least two hours.

Before serving, add two roughly chopped hard-boiled eggs to the soup, and sprinkle the surface with a little more black pepper and fresh herbs.

The taste is extraordinary, the different flavour and textures of the ingredients being preserved quite intact and independent by the yoghourt.

PLATE 5

PLATE 6 (see p. 129 for identification)

PLATE 7 (see p. 144 for identification)

PLATE 8 (see p. 145 for identification)

Wild angelica *Angelica sylvestris* [A] **Pl. 6**

Local names: GHOST-KEX, Yks; GROUND ASH, N. Eng; GROUND
ELDER, Ches; JACK-JUMP-ABOUT, N'thants; JEELICO, N. Eng;
KEDLOCK, Ches; KEWSIES, Lincs; SKYTES, Scot; SMOOTH
KESH, Cumb; SPOOTS, Shet; WATER SQUIRT, Som.

Widespread and common in damp woods, fens, and wet, grassy
places. Occurs throughout the British Isles. Flowers July to
September. A tall, stately umbelliferate, with hollow stems up to
5' high. The broad umbels of flowers are usually tinged with pink.
Leaves usually in groups of three or five, broad, toothed.

A close relative of garden angelica, *Angelica archangelica*, thinner
and more bitter than the cultivated variety, but good enough as a
flavouring. This is another plant about which some care should be
taken in identification. Its chief distinguishing features are the tall,
downy, hollow stems; the broad, toothed leaves; and the large
flower heads, which looks as if they have been 'dipped in claret'.

You will find wild angelica anywhere there is a combination of
wet and light – damp woodland rides and the edges of brooks are
favourite habitats. Cut some of the thickest stems and leaves
together, so that you have an adequate section for identification
when you get to a reliable field guide. The chopped leaves are
good with stewed fruit, especially rhubarb.

Angelica is best-known, of course, for its candied stems, and
though this is not a strictly herbal use, and you will not get such
good results as you will with the garden variety, it is worth a try.
Slice the stems into four inch lengths, scrape off any tough outside
fibres, and then simmer in sugar syrup until tender. Drain off the
syrup, strew crushed sugar over the stems and simmer again until

this thicker syrup is clear. Lift the stems on to a tray, boil up the syrup to sugar point, pour over the angelica; then drain, boil and pour again, repeating the cycle until the stems can be dried into firm, crystallised lengths.

Sweet gale *Myrica gale* [A]   Pl. 6

Local names: BOG MYRTLE. CANDLE BERRIES, Som; FLEA-WOOD, N'thum; GOLD-WITHY, Hants, IoW; GOLDEN OSIER, IoW; MOSS WYTHAN, Cumb; SWEET, Yks; SWEET WILLOW, Suss; WITHYWIND, Hants.

Locally common in bogs, marshes and wet heaths, mainly in Scotland, Ireland, N Wales and the SW of England. Flowers April to May. A deciduous shrub, 2' to 4' high with red and orange, (female and male) catkins on separate plants. These flowers appear before the leaves, which are grey-green, narrow, toothed, on shiny reddish twigs.

Before the extensive draining of the fens, sweet gale must have been a much more widespread plant. Now it is only locally common, but where it is, its leaves and flowers can scent the whole area with their delightfully sweet, resinous smell.

Gale was traditionally used for the flavouring of beer before hops were introduced to this country. There is evidence that this drink was being brewed in Anglo-Saxon times, and the isolated patches which grow around old monasteries and other early settlements suggest that it was occasionally taken into cultivation, outside its natural habitats.

Making gale beer is an elaborate business, but well worth the effort if you live near any of the areas where it grows.

Pack a jar or tub full of gale leaves. Measure how much water it will hold in order just to cover the leaves. Put half that amount of water on to boil, mixed with honey in the proportions of $\frac{1}{2}$ pint honey to one gallon of water. Once the liquid is boiling, pour it over the gale leaves, pressing them well down. Then add roughly the same quantity of boiling water again (without honey) so that your tub is full. Allow to cool to blood heat, and then stir in sufficient yeast to make the mixture start frothing noticeably.

Remove the gale and allow the beer to 'work' for about a week. Skim off the froth, and strain the beer into a wooden cask or strong stone jar. (DON'T try bottling it as it may still be fermenting and you will end up with some dangerously exploding bottles.) Leave the stopper or bung out for a day in case the transfer has started the working again. The beer will be ready to drink in about a month, but is better left until the first frost.

Corn mint *Mentha arvensis*   [A]   **Pl. 6**

Local names: APPLE MINT, Ire; LAMBS' TONGUES, Scot.

Widespread and frequent in arable land, heaths, damp woodland rides. Flowers June to September. A hairy, soft, pale green mint 3″ to 1½″ high. Leaves oval and toothed, in opposed pairs up the stalk, with the lilac flowers forming a ring at each junction.

Another much maligned plant, whose smell has been described as 'acrid' by one writer and like 'wet, mouldy gorgonzola' by Geoffrey Grigson. You must judge for yourself. It is coarser, certainly, than any of the cultivated mints, but once inside a sauce I don't find it much less refreshing.

The leaves are the same pale, soft green as the young shoots of garden mint, and can be picked at any time between April and September. If you are gathering mint at a time when there are no flowers visible, the smell of the crushed leaves will instantly confirm its identity. No other group of British plants has this distinctive smell.

Corn mint can be used exactly as if it were a garden mint. But if you should find its taste a little too bitter, even in a well-sugared mint sauce, try this recipe for Indian mint chutney, in which the wild mint's sharper qualities can be a positive virtue.

Wash and dry about 2 oz mint leaves, and grind to a thick paste with a quarter of a cupful of vinegar. (A liquidiser will do the job just as well.) Chop up quarter of a pound of tamarind (obtainable from most delicatessens), 2 oz green chillies (less if you do not like hot chutneys), a good sized onion and a clove of garlic. Add these ingredients, plus a dessertspoonful of salt, to the mint paste and mix thoroughly. Bottle and store for a few days before using.

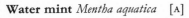

Water mint *Mentha aquatica* [A]

Local names: BISHOPWEED, Hants; HORSE MINT, Som, IoW, Glos, War, Lincs, Yks, N'thum; LILAC-FLOWER, Som.

Widespread and common by the edges of streams, in damp meadows, and woods, throughout the British Isles. Flowers July to September. A rough, hairy mint, often growing in quite sizeable clumps up to 2′ high. The leaves are frequently tinged with purple, and grow in opposed pairs. The bluish-lilac flowers grow chiefly in a round bushy head at the top of the plant.

This, our commonest waterside mint, has a flavour very reminiscent of peppermint (*Mentha piperita* p. 134 which is in fact a cross between this variety and spearmint, *Mentha spicata*). It often grows quite abundantly near water, its leaves immensely varied in size and coloration, but always crowned with a fine bush of lilac flowers.

It is cleaner and more piercing in smell and flavour than corn mint, and better as an addition to cooked dishes. John Gerard was a great fan: 'The savour or smell of the water mint rejoiceth the hart of man'. What better way to make use of this than that cool Transatlantic drink Mint Julep? Wash a bunch of mint, put it in a basin and bruise it with the back of a spoon. Add one cup of sugar, one tin of pineapple juice and the juice of four lemons. Stir the mixture well and allow to stand for about four or five hours. Strain into a jug, and add three bottles of dry ginger ale, ice cubes, some thin slices of lemon and a very few sprigs of fresh mint.

There are so many well-known uses for the more aromatic mints in cooking, that I cannot resist the temptation to give here the recipe for a real mint folly: mint and marshmallow custard. Beat together three eggs and a tablespoonful of sugar in a casserole. Gradually stir in one pint of milk. Float on the surface three teaspoons of chopped water mint, and on top of this, about 24 marshmallows. Stand the dish in a shallow tray of hot water, and bake in a moderate oven until set.

If you cannot face this, try adding mint to your cooked egg and cheese dishes as well as to the peas and spuds.

There are over a dozen varieties of mint growing wild in the British Isles, most of them quite rare. The following are the most interesting in culinary terms.

Corsican mint *Mentha requienii* [c]

A very rare mint, naturalised in a few woodland rides.

Pennyroyal *Mentha pulegium* [c]

Very uncommon on damp heaths in south-west England. Another herbalist's cure-all. Its two chief uses were apparently for repelling fleas and inducing births! A more reasonable use, given the carminative properties of many of the *Mentha* family's volatile oils, was in gripe water. Our forbears plainly had some serious digestive problems to judge from the potency of this recipe:

Take of pennyroyal ten handfuls, coriander seeds, aniseed, sweet fennel seeds, caraway seeds, of each one ounce; bruise them and put them to the herbs in an earthen pot; sprinkle on them a pint of brandy; let them stand all night. . . .

The English Hus-Wife, Gervase Markham

Whorled mint *Mentha verticillata* [c]

Widespread and not uncommon in damp places. Many members of the mint family hybridise readily with each other, and this species is a cross between our two commonest mints, *Mentha arvensis*, and *Mentha aquatica*.

Eau-de-Cologne mint *Mentha citrata* [c]

Very rare in the South of England. Has an aroma distinctly reminiscent of eau-de-Cologne.

Spearmint *Mentha spicata* [c]

Widespread but extremely local, and often simply an escape. This is the common garden mint.

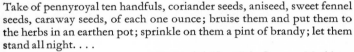

133

Peppermint *Mentha piperita* [C]

Uncommon in the south and west. This mint occurs only rarely in the wild, yet it is a natural hybrid between spearmint, *Mentha spicata*, and water mint, *Mentha aquatica*. It was not discovered in this country until the late seventeenth century. But why *peppermint*? It has a sharp taste, certainly, but nothing like the fieriness of pepper. The herb is now extensively cultivated for its aromatic oil, which is used in toothpastes, sweets, and indigestion remedies.

Horse-mint *Mentha longifolia* [C]

Widespread throughout the British Isles, but very local, by streams. Not unlike a mild spearmint in flavour and smell.

Apple mint *Mentha rotundifolia* [C]

Rare, except in the South and West, where it grows occasionally by roadsides. As the name suggests this mint smells strongly of apples.

Common calamint *Calamintha ascendens* [C]

Quite common locally on grassy banks in the southern parts of the British Isles, particularly on chalk and limestone. The smell and flavour resemble a cross between mint and marjoram.

Marjoram *Origanum vulgare* [A]   **Pl. 6**

Local names: JOY OF THE MOUNTAIN, Som; ORGAN, Dev, Wilts, Worc.

Widespread and locally common in grassy places on chalk and limestone. Rare in Scotland. Flowers July to October. A slender herb, growing up to three feet high, with downy stems extensively branched near the top of the plant. The leaves are oval and usually untoothed, and the flowers a pale, pinkish purple, in bunches at the head of the plant.

The marjoram which grows wild in this country is often known as oregano. It is spicier than sweet marjoram, *Origanum majorana*, but is still one of our most pleasantly fragrant herbs. In summer its flowers are alive with bees, who would appear to have a better opinion of our native herbs than us. We scarcely ever use the herb, but in the Mediterranean it is much valued as a flavouring for the more earthy, country dishes.

When you find marjoram growing wild on a dry heath or chalky roadside bank, its flimsy, slightly grey-tinted leaves look exceedingly appetising, and used raw they do indeed make a pleasantly pungent addition to salads. For use as a herb, pick some sprigs of the plant, flowers and all, whilst it is in full bloom. Later strip off the leaves and blossoms from the rather wiry stalk.

Wild marjoram is paramountly a meat herb. It gives a fine savour to stews and casseroles, to spaghetti sauces and shepherd's pie, even to grilled steaks, if they are first rubbed with the herb. But one of the most interesting recipes for the freshly picked plant is olives oregano. When olives are steeped in a marinade of flavoured oil, they acquire something of the aroma of the herb.

To one pound of pricked olives in a jar, add one cup of olive oil, one teaspoon of thyme, one teaspoon of crushed peppercorns, and three teaspoons of chopped wild marjoram. Close the jar, shake well and leave in a refrigerator for at least two days. Olives treated like this make a perfect centrepiece for a lunch for the season when marjoram is in flower. Serve them with a light red wine and cheese.

Wild marjoram becomes sweeter as it dries and can then be used in a wider range of dishes. One unusual recipe is for herb scones, to be served with roasted meat. Rub 2 oz of butter into 4 oz of salted flour. Add a heaped teaspoon of dried marjoram, and enough cold water to make a stiff dough. Mix well but lightly with a knife, and then shape into thin cakes with your hand. Put these on a greased tray in the oven for about quarter of an hour (longer if you are cooking the meat slowly).

Wild thyme *Thymus drucei* [A]   **Pl. 6**

Local names: BANK THYME, Berks; HORSE THYME, N'thants; MOTHER OF THYME, Worc, Cumb, Ire; SHEPHERD'S THYME, Glos, Bucks, Oxf, Worc, War.

Widespread and often abundant in grassy places, especially on chalk and limestone, and on sandy heaths. Uncommon in the south-east. Flowers June to August. A prostrate, creeping plant, with rather woody stems and runners. Leaves very small, oval, and ranged in many opposing pairs along the stalks. The flowers are reddish purple in roundish bunches at the ends of the stalks.

Wild thyme is a herb of open places. It grows abundantly on grassy mountain approaches, on what is left of our chalk downlands, and even on dry roadside banks in the uplands. But be under no illusions: your nostrils are not going to be filled with that heady aroma as you stride over the springy turf with your basket. Wild thyme has neither the bushy forthrightness nor the pungency of cultivated thyme, *Thymus vulgaris*. It is a subtle, skulking plant, often growing entirely below grass level. Finding it is a hands-and-knees job, a rummage through the miniature downland flora, the milkworts and violets, for one sprig of toy, oval leaves that yield that clovy smell between the fingers. Then, tracing the runners back, following their meanderings through the dry lower stems of the grasses back to the woody root.

For the short while each plant is in flower, picking is a simpler exercise – though less rewarding I think than the inch by inch ferreting for the spring and autumn shoots. The flower heads are large compared to the size of the plant, and like marjoram conspicuous for their attendant insects. Wild thyme is best picked when in full bloom, so that the honey-scented flowers can be used as well as the leaves.

If you like you can strip the leaves and flowers off the stalk before using. But as wild thyme is considerably milder than the garden variety you can afford to use large sprigs of it liberally – and indeed to try it out in unconventional combinations. The great virtue of wild thyme is precisely its versatility. I can remember it even coming to the rescue of an ill-assorted collection of beef and remnant vegetables left over at the end of a Welsh canal holiday. It was our last day, and we had set off to look for stray red kites on Skirrid Fawr. We found no kites but a great deal of wild thyme, and back on the boat we stuffed meat, veg and swathes of the herb inside some foil and let it all seethe in the oven. The result was delectable, a tender pot-roast scented right through with the subtle, earthy fragrance of the wild thyme.

Garden thyme, even in relatively small quantities, would have quite overpowered beef cooked in this way. This is partly due to the greater concentration of thyme's characteristic volatile oil, thymol, in the cultivated variety. (Did our ancestors have some inkling of the antiseptic properties of this oil? Thyme was a key herb in both the Judge's posy and the Sovereign's Maundy Thursday posy, devices it was hoped would afford their carriers protection from the infectious diseases of the poor.) But wild thyme can be quite safely used in any of the recipes which include its stronger relative. It goes well with many vegetables, particularly mushrooms and courgettes, and in stuffings for poultry, veal and lamb. A dish which makes good use of the herb is savoury meat balls in sauce. Simmer together for about fifteen minutes one and a half pints of water, one onion, a bay leaf, a few peppercorns, some salt and two beef cubes. Remove the onion and the bay leaf. Then add to the sauce some meat balls formed out of 1½ lbs of sausage meat, one beaten egg, a chopped onion, two teaspoonfuls of dried thyme and a little seasoning. Simmer for half an hour. Remove the meat balls from the sauce, and thicken the latter with a dessertspoon of cornflour blended with a little milk. Replace the meat balls, warm and serve.

Woodruff *Galium odoratum* [A] **Pl. 6**

Local names: BLOOD CUP, Dor; KISS-ME-QUICK, Dor, Som; LADIES-IN-THE-HAY, Wilts; LADY'S NEEDLEWORK, Som; MADDER, Wilts; NEW-MOWN-HAY, Som, Notts; RICE FLOWER, Som; ROCKWOOD, Dev; SCENTED HAIRHOOD, Yks; STAR-GRASS, Cumb, N'thum; SWEETGRASS, Berw; SWEETHEARTS, Som; WOODREP, Scot; WOOD-ROWELL, Yks.

Widespread and often abundant in woods and thick hedgerows, especially beech, and on chalk and limestone. Flowers April to June, small, white and four-petalled, in loose heads. Grows in clusters to about 1' high, with whorls of six to nine leaves at intervals up the smooth stems.

In the late spring, the edges of beech woods are often thickly carpeted with the young shoots of woodruff, immaculate in their tiny marble-white flowers and brisk green ruffs. When they are green the plants are almost odourless; but allow them to dry and they quickly develop the cool, fresh smell of new mown hay. Indeed, the plant was once popular for scenting dried linen and laying in beds.

This smell, which you will recognise if you have ever dried meadowsweet or melilot, is due to a chemical called coumarin (from which, incidentally, some of the latest anti-coagulant drugs used in heart disease are derived). The scent readily transfers to liquids, and makes dried woodruff an ideal herb to add to summer wine cups. A bottle of pure apple juice in which a sprig has been allowed to steep for a week or so, becomes positively ambrosial.

Fenugreek *Trigonella ornithopodioides* [C]   **Pl. 6**

Another coumarin-scented plant, fenugreek is a pink-flowered member of the pea family which grows infrequently in dry sandy places, especially near coasts in the southern half of England.

The fenugreek whose leaves and exceedingly hard, irregularly-shaped seeds are used in Indian cookery, is not this plant but its close relative, *trigonella foenum-graecum,* a native of the Mediterranean. But English fenugreek is aromatic when dry and worth experimenting with in a similar way.

Sweet cicely *Myrrhis odorata* [C]

Cicely is one of the few plants where the connotation 'sweet' refers as much to taste as to smell. The feathery leaves have distinctly sugary overtones to their mild aniseed flavour, and are ideal for flavouring stewed fruits such as gooseberries and plums. Some experimenters have been able to halve the amount of sugar they would normally use for such dishes by the plentiful addition of the herb.

Sadly it is not a common plant, but small colonies can often be found by grassy roadsides in Scotland and the North. Its foliage is magnificently extravagant, sometimes growing up to 5' tall, and it is surprising that the plant is not cultivated more often in gardens. Gerard was very much in favour of sweet cicely, and wrote that its leaves were 'exceedingly good, holsome, and pleasant among other sallade herbes, giving the taste of Anise seed unto the rest'. He also ate the roots boiled like parsnips, and – did Gerard really not think much of his own cooking? – 'dressed how the cunning Cooke knoweth better than myself'.

There seems no end to the uses which can be found for this plant. It is one of the herbs which are used in the making of Chartreuse, and in Westmorland the leaves were used to polish oak panels.

Parsley *Petroselinum crispum* [C]

It is doubtful whether any of the parsley plants which can occasionally be found growing wild on rocky places near the sea, are any more than escapees from gardens. The plant is almost certainly a comparatively recent introduction from the Mediterranean, and I can find no records of it being grown here before the sixteenth century.

As a change from a redundant garnishing, try frying your parsley for half a minute in hot butter, and serving it as a vegetable with fish. It is extremely rich in Vitamin C.

Lovage *Ligusticum scoticum* [C]

A stocky umbelliferate with bright green, leathery leaves, which grows locally on rocky sea cliffs in Scotland. It was occasionally eaten against scurvy.

Its cultivated cousin, *Ligusticum officinale*, is naturalised from herb gardens in a few places. This domesticated lovage is a much more distinctive plant, growing six or seven feet tall, and its uses are correspondingly wider. The hollow stems have been candied like angelica, and blanched like celery for use as a salad vegetable.

The flavour of both varieties is curious, basically resembling celery, but having quite strong yeasty overtones. Because of this lovage has been used to add body to the flavour of soups and casseroles when meat is short.

Borage *Borago officinalis*   [c]   Pl. 6

Borage once had a great reputation as a sort of herbal pep-pill. It was renowned as an aphrodisiac and as a general dispeller of melancholy and depression. John Evelyn clearly understood the type of person who would perennially be in need of such aids when he wrote that 'the sprigs . . . are of known virtue to revive the hypochondriac and cheer the hard student'. I can testify to one case, at least, where the dried leaves proved of inestimable value as a hangover cure, used first as an inhalant in hot water and then, in desperation, drunk. It really did seem to have a remarkably exhilarating and head-clearing effect.

Whatever its medicinal qualities, the young leaves and bright blue, star-like flowers make a refreshing and fragrant addition to claret cups and other summer drinks, particularly in combination with woodruff.

But you will be lucky to find any truly wild borage to use in this way. It occurs only very rarely in the wild, and then usually as an escapee.

Wild basil *Clinopodium vulgare*   [c]   Pl. 6

The plant which goes under the name of wild basil in this country is unfortunately only a distant relative of the well-known garden herb, sweet basil, *Ocimum basilicum*. It's rough in texture as well as flavour and only very slightly aromatic. Yet it does grow plentifully on heaths and other dry, grassy places, and shouldn't be overlooked if other herbs are scarce. It is a cheery little plant, downy and upright, and crowned with a dome-shaped whorl of pinkish-purple flowers from which the plant gets its other name 'cushion calamint'.

Since the plant is rather coarse and woolly, use only the leaves, well-chopped, in cooked dishes. They are too rough to be used in salads, like sweet basil, and seem to lose what flavour they have on drying. Try the herb with cooked fungi dishes, and in sauces containing tomato (like that for spaghetti bolognaise).

Balm *Melissa officinalis* [C]

Another introduced herb, naturalised in a few places in the south of England. Balm is an undistinguished plant much like a bushy mint, yet it was very popular in Elizabethan gardens. Bees adore the flowers, and it was reputed that they would never leave a garden that had a clump of them growing. While a bee-hive was still a standard fixture in gardens, so was a bee-balm.

It was also grown for its lemon-scented leaves, which flavoured wines and teas. When lemons were scarce they were sometimes used to give a tang of apple jelly, and added to stuffings and salads.

Ground ivy *Glechoma hederacea* [C]

The dried leaves of ground ivy make one of the more agreeable herbal teas, cooling and with a sharp, slight fragrance. The flower is common in woods (especially oak) and hedgebanks, and often occurs in gardens.

Before hops became widely accepted in the seventeenth century, ground ivy – known then as alehoof – was one of the chief agents for flavouring and clarifying ale. Culpeper wrote of it: 'It is good to tun up with new drink, for it will clarify it in a night, that it will be fitter to be dranke the next morning; or if any drinke be thick with removing or any other accident, it will do the like in a few hours'.

Lady's bedstraw *Galium verum* [C]

Lady's bedstraw is a feathery, insubstantial plant, whose myriads of tiny yellow flowers smell of honey when cool and fresh. But when the plant is dried it develops the characteristic hay-like smell of coumarin (like woodruff, also a member of the bedstraw family). Coumarin breaks down to yield a powerful anti-coagulant, dicoumarol, and there is always a small quantity of this in picked specimens of the plant. Yet lady's bedstraw must also contain some enzyme-like substance which overrides this, as it is of proven value as a styptic, and for curdling milk into junkets and cheese. I have never found full instructions for this old practice, and have not yet succeeded in making more than a thin skin of rather bitter junket with it. But experiment with different consistencies of milk, different temperatures and parts of the plant, and see if you can rediscover the recipe.

Tansy *Chrysanthemum vulgare* [C]   **Pl. 6**

There was a time when tansy was probably the most widely grown garden herb of all. It was a key item in the housewife's armoury of medicines, and had an extraordinarily wide range of uses in the kitchen. All of which goes to show how much our tastes have changed over the last few centuries, for even by the fairly tolerant standards I have tried to apply in this book, tansy is an unusually off-putting plant. It smells like a strong chest-ointment and has a hot, bitter taste. Used in excess it is more than unpleasant, and can be a dangerous irritant to the stomach.

Nevertheless, at Easter the young leaves were traditionally served with fried eggs and used to flavour puddings made from milk, flour and eggs. This may have been to symbolise the bitter herbs eaten by the Jews at Passover, though one sixteenth century writer explained that it was to counteract the effects 'engendered of Fish in the Lent season'. He may have been on to something, as the quality of fish at that time no doubt gave much room for the development of worms, and Oil of Tansy is quite effective as a vermifuge.

Earlier still, the juice was extracted from the chopped leaves and used to flavour omelettes. This gave the name 'Tansye' in the fifteenth century as a generic term for any herb-flavoured omelette. And there was a delightful medieval bubble-and-squeak, made from a fry-up of tansy leaves, green corn, and violets, and served with orange and sugar.

Try the taste of tansy for yourself. Whatever you think of its flavour it is an attractive little plant with its golden, button-shaped flowers and ferny leaves.

Wormwood *Artemisia absinthium* [C]

A bitter oil extracted from the flower-heads of this attractive silky-grey plant is the key ingredient of absinthe, that most potent of alcoholic drinks. The flowers have also been used on the Continent to counteract the greasiness of goose and duck dishes. Used in small quantities the herb has beneficial, tonic properties. But in excess it can be damaging to the heart. It also contains an anthelmintic (worm-dispeller) called santonin, which is a hallucinogen if taken in overdose. Objects first appear blue and then change to yellow.

All the *Artemisias* contain small quantities of this rather disturbing substance, including the feathery sea wormwood, *Artemisia maritima*, and the common roadside mugwort, *Artemisia vulgaris*, which have both been used occasionally in the same ways as wormwood.

Sand leek *Allium scorodoprasum* [C]

This close relative of garlic – sometimes called 'rocambole' – grows very locally in hedge-banks and rough grass in N. England and southern Scotland. The plant has occasionally been taken into cultivation, or gathered in the wild state, and the bulbs and stems used in the same way as garlic.

Chives *Allium schoenoprasum* [C]

Although chives is properly a native of Northern Europe, it does grow rarely in the wild in Great Britain, mainly on limestone cliffs near fresh water.

Chives has long been cultivated as a herb, being especially prized by those who like the characteristic flavour of onions, but only in moderation. Its mildness and almost complete absence of a bulb have earned chives the name of 'Infant Onion'.

It is a highly adaptable herb, going well with cream cheese, potatoes, cucumber, salads and omelettes.

Ramsons *Allium ursinum* [C]   **Pl. 6**

I have given ramsons a C rating because it really is a bewitchingly attractive plant, with its cluster of brilliant white, star-like flowers and lily-of-the-valley leaves. But it is quite widespread in Britain, in dark hedges and damp woods, and where it is growing abundantly the loss of the few leaves would not be too serious.

For those who like their garlic strong, ramsons will prove magnetic. Every part of the plant smells quite overpoweringly, especially when it has been bruised by picking. Even wrapped in newspaper and banished to the boot of your car, you will still find you need to travel with the windows open. Yet curiously, as with so many wild herbs, much of this pungency vanishes on cooking, and the chopped leaves can be used as a way of giving a very mild garlic flavour to a dish.

Gerard reports that in some parts of Europe a sauce for fish was made from the leaves, which may also 'very well be eaten in April and May with butter, of such as are of strong constitution, and labouring men'.

In dire circumstances both wild garlic, *Allium oleraceum*, and crow garlic, *Allium vineale*, have also been used as flavourings.

Spices

For the purposes of this section, spices are the aromatic seeds of flowering plants. There are a few roots (e.g. galingale and horse-radish) that are generally regarded as spices, but I have described these in the chapter on roots.

Most plants which have aromatic leaves also have aromatic seeds, and the seeds of most of the plants in the herbs section can be usefully employed as flavourings. But a warning: do not expect the flavour of the two parts to be identical. They are often subtly different in ways that make it inadvisable simply to substitute seeds for leaves.

Seeds should always be allowed to dry on the plant. After flowering, annuals start to concentrate their food supplies into the seeds so that they have enough to survive through germination. This also, of course, increases the flavour and size of the seeds. When they are dry and ready to drop off the plant, their food content and flavour should be at a maximum.

Never take any of the seeds of an uncommon plant, or too many even from the commoner annuals. If you do there is a good chance that next year there will be no plants for you to crop or others to see.

Corn poppy, Field poppy *Papaver rhoeas* [A]   **Pl. 7**

Local names: numerous, including: BLIND EYES, N'thants; CANKER, Suff, Norf; CHEESEBOWLS, Som; EARACHES, Derb, Notts; GYE, Suff; HEADACHE, Som, Suss, E Ang, N'thants,

Ches, Derb, Leic, Notts, Rut, Lincs, Yks, Cumb, Ire; PEPPER BOXES, Som; POISON POPPY, Bucks; POPPET, War; REDWEED, Dor, Som, Wilts, Hants, IoW, Suss, Kent, Berks, Bucks, Herts, Norf, E. Ang; SLEEPYHEAD, Som; THUNDERBOLT, Dev, W. Eng, Shrop, Ches.

Widespread and abundant in arable field and by roadsides. Becomes scarcer in Wales, N.W. England, and N. Scotland. Flowers June to October, deep scarlet, floppy petals at the top of a thin, hairy stalk, one to two feet high. The seed-pods are hairless, and flat-topped like an inverted cone.

It was once believed that smelling poppies gave you a headache, that staring at them for too long made you go blind. Superstitions about the supposed poisonousness of the flower still persist, notably the belief that the seed heads contain opium. In fact no parts of the common field poppy are narcotic, least of all the dry seeds. It is *Papaverum somniferum* from which opium is derived by the cutting and draining of the unripe seed heads.

Once poppies and cornfields were inseparable. Even the Romans' corn goddess, Ceres, was depicted with a bundle of poppies in one hand. Now herbicides and the treating of seed have virtually eliminated them from arable fields. Yet they can still be found, sometimes in great abundance, swaying by the sides of roads and in gardens and waste places.

The seed heads start to dry in September, and are ready for picking when they are grey-brown in colour, and have a number of small holes just below the edge of the flat top. (These are vents through which the seeds normally escape.) The seed in ripe heads can be readily shaken out of these holes.

Pick a handful of these heads, and put them straight into a paper bag. Remove the seeds by inverting the heads and shaking them into the bag. Any that cling onto their contents are not really ripe.

Poppy seeds are slate grey in colour and have an elusive taste. They are extensively used in European and Middle Eastern cookery, particularly for sprinkling on bread, rolls, cakes and biscuits. But they also go well with honey as a dressing for fruit, and with noodles and macaroni.

Black mustard *Brassica nigra* [C] Pl. 7

The awl-shaped seed pods of black mustard begin to ripen in August. You will need to gather a large number to use them seriously, but the seeds have an intriguing taste, not at all as harsh as might be expected, and are worth nibbling even if your patience stops short at picking enough to cook with.

Each pod will contain three or four oblong, reddish-brown seeds. It is these which are ground up for commercial mustards, being mixed with various combinations of white mustard seed, (*Sinapis alba*) turmeric, vinegar, flour and other spices.

Medieval mustard was more like a salad dressing than our thick yellow paste. John Evelyn gives the following instructions:

Take the mustard seed, and grind one and a half pints of it with honey, and Spanish oil, and make it into a liquid sauce with vinegar. . . .

To make mustard for the pot, slice some horse-radish, and lay it to soak in vinegar, squeezing it well, and add a lump of sugar and an onion chopt. Use the vinegar from this mixture to mix the mustard.

Acetaria

However the mustard was prepared its traditional use was as an accompaniment to beef. In *Midsummer Night's Dream*, Bottom cannot resist teasing Master Mustard-seed with this association: 'I know your patience well: that same cowardly, giant-like ox-beef hath devoured many a gentleman of your house. I promise you, your kindred hath made my eyes water ere now.' Even if you only gather a handful of pods the best use you can make of the seeds is probably with steak, pressing them into the surface before grilling. Small quantities can also be used up in Welsh Rarebits, salads and sauces.

But if you should succeed in gathering enough pods to yield an oz of seeds, try this lemon and mustard seed chutney. It is worth cheating for, and *buying* your mustard seed if necessary!

Peel and slice four medium-sized onions, slice five lemons thinly and discard the pips. Mix, sprinkle with salt and leave for twelve hours. Add one oz of mustard seed, one teaspoon of ground allspice, one lb sugar, one quarter of a pound of seedless raisins, and a pint of cider vinegar. Bring to the boil and simmer for about an hour. Transfer to jars and seal when cool.

Coriander *Coriandrum sativum* [C]   **Pl. 7**

When you come across a green coriander plant, it is difficult to believe that it will eventually produce those warmly aromatic seeds that are used so extensively in curries. The odour of the fresh plant is positively foetid; in fact its name, *Coriandrum*, derives from the Greek word for bug.

Coriander grows wild in a few scattered places in the British Isles (even alongside the M1), and was probably brought here from its native Mediterranean habitat by the Romans. The dried seeds are mentioned in Exodus, and are one of the oldest spices known to man. Ground up, they are an essential ingredient of most curries, and will add a subtle flavour to casseroles, soups, and especially pork dishes. Len Deighton's recommendation: 'Hurl crushed coriander seeds into any open pot you see'.

Caraway *Carum carvi* [C]

Caraway is probably a genuine native in one or two sites in the British Isles. But it is an extremely rare umbelliferate, and most specimens found in the wild are escapes from cultivation. Every part of the plant has been used for food at some time. But it is the seeds that are best known and for which the plant is cultivated. An oil extracted from them is a recognised treatment for indigestion, and is also used to flavour Kümmel liqueur. The seeds themselves are added to cakes and bread, and have given their name to seed-cake. They are also the classic flavouring added to cabbage as it is being salted down to sauerkraut.

Flowers

Over-picking is seriously affecting the populations of many of our wild flowers. Bluebells, primroses and cowslips in particular have been drastically reduced in areas that are well worked by tourists. It is not just that every flower picked is one less to see and, looked at severely, is an act of theft from the public; it is that the plants can be irreparably damaged by rough picking, and even more by the heavy feet of the pickers. Gathering flowers for no other reason than their diverting flavours could hardly be looked at as an exception.

The only species I have included in category A, and therefore actually recommended for use, all have certain characteristics which make the picking of their flowers in small quantities unlikely to have much visual or biological effect. They are all very common and hardy plants. They are all perennials and do not rely on seeding for continued survival. They are all bushes or shrubs in which each individual produces an abundant number of blossoms.

Many other species have been used in the past and by all accounts been found attractive eating. I have included these for completeness' sake, but unless they fulfil the criteria I have given above, they have been relegated to category C. You will find there common species like the violet alongside rarer ones like the chamomile; I would hope that they would all be regarded as forbidden, and left to blossom for everyone's delight. (If you have them growing in the privacy of your garden, then it is another matter.)

A few notes on how to minimise the effect of picking even on the comparatively invulnerable A entries:

1. Do not take more than a few flower heads from each bush. The best rule is to leave each plant looking the same as you found it.
2. Cut them with a knife or scissors to minimise the damage to the plant.

3. Pick rather less than you think you need. None of the recipes given on the following pages need much more than a couple of handfuls of blossoms.

To get the best out of the flowers you do pick, gather them into a flat basket to prevent squashing, and use them as soon as possible after picking.

There was, incidentally, a general medieval recipe for flowers which consisted of boiling the blossoms, chopping them, and then mixing with milk, ground almonds, sugar and honey.

Lime *Tilia europaea* [A]

(For details see p. 79)

In late June and July the yellow flowers of mature lime trees have a delicious honey-like fragrance, and make one of the very best teas of all wild flowers. It is popular in France where it is sold under the name of *tilleul*.

The flowers should be gathered whilst they are in full bloom, and laid out on trays in a warm, well-ventilated room to dry. After two or three weeks they are ready for use. Make tea from them in the usual way, experimenting with strengths, and serve like China tea, without milk.

It is nice to think that this homely drink has been recognised to have sedative properties and was used by doctors during the Second World War as a mild tranquilliser.

Broom *Sarothamnus scoparius* [A]   Pl. 7

Local names: BANADLE, Wales; BASOM, Corn, Dev, Som; BRUSHER, Dor; CAT'S PEAS, Corn; GOLDEN CHAIR, Dor, Som; LADY'S SLIPPER, Som.

Widespread and often abundant on heaths, sandy places and dry, acid soils. Flowers May to June. A hairless bush, growing up to five feet high, with long sprays of willowy, spineless branches and an abundance of brilliant yellow, pea-shaped flowers.

In early summer many heathy places are ablaze with broom, quite out-shining the gorse it normally grows with. The great banks of golden flowers smell of ripe peaches, and can be so dense and brilliant that they actually reflect the heat of the sun.

Broom has always been a plant of great economic usefulness. Bunches of the fine, whippy twigs had an obvious domestic use, and gave their name to the universal sweeping instrument. The young green shoots, broom tops, are used as a mild diuretic and heart tonic. But there is still a good deal of superstitious belief in the magical and poisonous qualities of broom. Does this date back to the time when witches used broomsticks (literally) in their rituals? Broom does contain minute quantities of certain alkaloids, but enormous quantities of the plant would need to be eaten to make it even slightly dangerous. Certainly the young flower buds – the parts which normally find their way into kitchens – can be used with complete confidence.

The buds can be picked from the branches in late April and May. They can be pickled or added to salads. In the sixteenth and seventeenth centuries they were a standard ingredient of Grand Salletts and Salmagundys, those extravagant, baroque concoctions that seemed to employ every conceivable taste, colour and texture in the kitchen. Here is a recipe from the early sixteen hundreds:

Cut cold roast chicken or other meats into slices. Mix with minced tarragon and an onion. Mix all together with capers, olives, samphire, broombuds, mushrooms, oysters, lemon, orange, raisins, almonds, blue figs, Virginia potatoes, peas, and red and white currants. Garnish with sliced oranges and lemons. Cover with oil and vinegar, beaten together.

adapted from *The Good Huswives Treasure*, Robert May, 1588–1660

How much more exciting than the wilted lettuce we often pass off as salad. One can imagine what these exhibition pieces looked like, laid out on huge plates, with the guarantee of a surprise in every forkful.

Wild rose, Dog rose *Rosa canina* [A]   Pl. 7

Local names: numerous, including BRIAR (very widespread); BRIMMLE, Shrop; CANKER, Dev, Dor, Som, Ess, Norf, Lincs, Cumb; CAT-WHIN, Yks, N. Eng; CHOOP-ROSE, Cumb; COCK-BRAMBLE, Suff; DIKE-ROSE, Cumb; HIP-TREE, Glos, N'thum;

HORSE-BRAMBLE, E. Ang; HUMACK, Som; LAWYERS, Surr, War; HEDDY-GRINNEL, Worc; PIG'S ROSE, Dev.

Widespread and common in hedges, scrubland, waste places, but less frequent in Scotland. Flowers June to July. A tall, sturdy shrub 4' to 10' high, with hooked prickles, toothed leaves, and large white to pink, five-petalled flowers.

The wild rose is England's national flower, and keeps its dignity even as it dies. There is none of the protracted wilting often shown by garden roses, which can hang sodden and wrinkled on their branches for days. The wild rose has a simpler and less showy blossom which scarcely even droops before it sheds its petals. This is the stage when they should be gathered. Never pick or damage the young flowers. Towards the end of July look for those that have already lost one or two petals, and then gently remove the others into your basket.

Roses of all sorts have always been one of man's favourite flowers. Rosaries themselves originally consisted of strings of beads made from the pressed petals. The Romans used to adorn their tables with them, and at one banquet apparently showered down so many petals from the ceiling that some of the guests were suffocated.

Wild roses have a more delicate scent than the garden varieties, but still some of that fleshy, perfumed texture. So if you have only a small quantity, use them neat in salads. Frances Perry once listed ten other uses for the petals: rose wine, rose in brandy, rose vinegar, rhubarb and rose-petal jam, rose honey, rose and coconut candies, Turkish delight, rose drops, crystallised rose petals, and rose-petal jelly. The list could be extended indefinitely, because the basis of the use of rose petals, here as elsewhere, is simply as a fragrant improver of well-established dishes. Rose-petal jam is extensively eaten in the Middle East, especially with yoghourt, and the recipe below is from Turkey. You will only need to prepare a small potful, as it is exceedingly sweet. And only supplement your wild petals with those from garden roses if it is absolutely necessary to make up the quantity: the thick, fleshy petals of the garden damasks are very difficult to reduce to jelly.

Take two cups of wild rose petals, and make sure that they are free of insects. (Cram them down fairly tightly into the cup when you measure.) Dissolve two cupfuls of sugar in half a cup of water, mixed with one tablespoon each of lemon juice and orange juice. Then stir in the rose petals and put the pan over a very low heat. Stir continuously for about half an hour, or until all the petals have melted. Cool a little, pour into a small glass jar and cover.

Hawthorn *Crataegus monogyna* [A]

(For details see p. 82)

May has a wickedly exciting, musky smell, and it's not surprising that it makes a fine liqueur. Cut the pink or white flowers with scissors, trying to gather as little as possible of the thin stalks. Pack them loosely into a wide-mouthed bottle and shake over them a couple of tablespoons of sugar. Fill the bottle up with brandy, cork, and store in a warm cupboard for at least three months. (During the first week or two shake the bottle occasionally so that the sugar is properly dissolved and distributed.) After this period decant or filter the liqueur into a small bottle and seal securely.

Hop *Humulus lupulus* [A]

(For details see p. 93)

The green, cone-like female flowers of the hop have been used for flavouring beer since the ninth century. Yet though the plant is a British native, hops were not used for brewing in this country until the fifteenth century. Even then there was considerable opposition to their addition to the old ale recipes, and it was another hundred years before hop-growing became a commercial operation.

Hops have proved something of a mixed blessing. They certainly improved the flavour of crude ales and enabled beer to be kept longer. Yet in doing this they opened the door to mass production techniques in brewing, a step which led inexorably to the indistinguishable, fizzy, metallic liquids we have to drink today.

Brewing, like breadmaking, was traditionally a job done at home, and perhaps as a reaction against the quality of commercial beer, it is increasingly being done so again. It is not an easy process, and I would advise readers to look through some of the many books on the subject, and find a recipe that suits their own equipment and patience. But the hops at least are easy to find. The plant can be found clambering around many damp hedges, and the flowers are ready for picking by mid-September. For strongly flavoured beers they are used fresh; dry them in a warm airing cupboard (or a very low oven) until they are pale brown, and they give a lighter brew.

Heather *Calluna vulgaris*   [A]   **Pl. 7**

Local names: LING, HADDER, E. Ang, Yks, West, Cumb; BASSOM, Corn, Dev; BROOM, Dev, Som, Bucks, Yks; GRIG, Corn, Norf, Heref, Shrop, Ches, Wales; GRIGLANS, Corn; MOUNTAIN MIST, Som.

Widespread and abundant on heaths, moors, and in dry open woods. Flowers August to September. A stubby, evergreen shrub, 6″ to 18″ high, with numerous tiny leaves in opposite rows. The flowers are purple and bell-shaped and carried in spikes.

Perhaps our most widely known wild flower. Heather is a tenacious and aggressive plant and completely carpets huge areas of moorland. Trample on it and you will make no impression on its wiry stems. Even extensive burning only sets it back temporarily, and within a couple of years new shoots spring up beside the blackened branches of the old.

Heather has an abundant range of economic uses. It provides food for sheep and grouse, material for fuel, thatching, basketwork and brooms, and an orange dye. In some places it was used for flavouring ale.

The dried flower heads make a good tea, and Robert Burns is supposed to have drunk a 'Moorland Tea' based on heather tops mixed with the dried leaves of bilberry, blackberry, speedwell, thyme, and wild strawberry.

Elder *Sambucus nigra*   [A]   **Pl. 7**

Local names: BOUR-TREE, Ches, Lincs, Lancs, Yks, Lakes, Dur, N'thum, Scot, N. Ire; BORRAL, N'thum, Scot; BULL-TREE,

Cumb; DEVIL'S WOOD, Derb; DOG-TREE, Yks; ELLER, Suss, Kent, Norf, Ches, Derb, Lincs, Yks, West, N. Eng; GOD'S STINKING TREE, Dor; JUDAS-TREE, Kent; SCAW, Corn; TEA-TREE, Som; TRAMMON, IoM.

Widespread and common in woods, hedgerows and waste places. Flowers June to July. A tall, fast-growing shrub, with a corky bark, white pith in the heart of the branches, and a scaly surface to the young twigs. Leaves usually in groups of five; large, dark-green and slightly toothed. Flowers: umbels of numerous tiny cream-white flowers.

To see the mangy, decaying skeletons of elders in the winter you would not think the bush was any use to man or beast. Nor would the acrid stench of the young leaves in spring change your opinion. But by the end of June the whole shrub is covered with great sprays of sweet-smelling flowers, for which there are probably more uses than any other single species of blossom. Even in orthodox medicine they have an acknowledged role as an ingredient in skin ointments and eye-lotions.

Elder flowers are good munched straight off the branch on a hot summer's day; they are as cool and frothy as a glass of ice-cream soda. Something even closer to that drink can be made by putting a bunch of elder flowers in a jug with boiling water, straining the liquid off when cool, and sweetening.

Cut the elder flower clusters whole, with about two inches of stem attached to them. (This is needed for one of the recipes.) Always check that they are free of insects, and discard any that are badly infested. The odd grub or two can be removed by hand. But never wash the flowers as this will remove much of the fragrance. The young buds can be pickled or added to salads. The flowers themselves, separated from the stalks, make what is indisputably the best sparkling wine besides champagne. But the two most famous recipes for elder flowers are the preserve they make with gooseberries and elder-flower fritters.

To make the preserve, trim off as much of the rather bitter stalk as you can, and have ready four flower heads for each pound of gooseberries. Top, tail and wash the gooseberries in the usual way, and put them into a pan with one pint of water for every pound of fruit. Simmer for half an hour, mashing the fruit to a pulp as you do. Add one pound of sugar for each pound of fruit, stir rapidly until dissolved, and bring to the boil. Then add the elder flowers, tied in muslin, and boil rapidly until the setting point is reached. Remove the flowers and pot in the usual way. (See p. 159 for a few extra notes on jams generally.) The flavour is quite transformed from that of plain gooseberry jam, and is reminiscent of muscat grapes. It is good with ice-cream and other sweets.

The fritters are made with a thin batter prepared from 4 tablespoons of flour, one egg and about 1½ cupfuls of water. Hold the flower heads by the stalks and dip into the batter. Strain off any excess, and then plunge into hot oil and deep-fry until golden brown. Trim off the excess stalk and serve with sugar and perhaps a little fresh mint. They make a perfect and delicately flavoured finish to a summer meal.

Sweet violet *Viola odorata* [C]   Pl. 7

The sweet violet is fairly common in hedgebanks and shady places in England and Wales, though less frequent than the almost odourless dog violet. In the past its flowers were used quite extensively in cooking for their fragrance and decorative qualities. They were one of the ingredients of the Salmagundy. In the fourteenth century they were beaten up with a ground rice pudding flavoured with ground almonds and cream. Much later, after émigrés from the French Revolution had made veal popular in this country, they were used as one of the elaborate floral dressings for joints of that meat. They are best known, though, as the crystallised sweets.

Cowslip *Primula veris* [C]

The cheerful, wobbly blossoms of the cowslip have made it one of our favourite flowers, and it has probably suffered more from over-picking than any other of our once common meadow flowers. Yet its name hardly suggests such popularity. It is a euphemism for 'cowslop', no doubt an indication of the plant's liking for mucky fields.

It was once widely used in kitchens, making one of the very best country wines, and a curious 'vinegar' which was drunk with soda water rather than being used as a condiment. (To show the devastation some of these recipes must have wreaked on flower populations, this particular recipe required two pints of cowslip blossoms to make a pint and a half of vinegar.)

Izaak Walton used cowslip blossoms (and primroses) as a flavouring for minnows:

He is a sharp biter at a small worm, and in hot weather makes excellent sport for young anglers, or boys, or women that love that recreation, and in the spring they make of them excellent minnow-tansies; for being washed well in salt, and their heads and tails cut off, and their guts taken out, and not washed after, they prove excellent for that use; that is, being fried with yolks of eggs, the flowers of cowslips, and of primroses, and a little tansy; thus used they make a dainty dish of meat.

The Compleat Angler, 5th ed., 1676

Primrose *Primula vulgaris* [c] **Pl. 7**

The symbol of spring, with its pure, pale, delicately fragrant yellow flowers and crinkly leaves. The primrose can grow abundantly on chalk banks, railway embankments, shady woods, even on cliffs, but it is greatly reduced near big towns and cities.

Primrose blossoms have mostly been used in identical ways to cowslips, for making drinks, and as a dressing for roast veal.

Common chamomile *Chamaemelum nobile* [c] **Pl. 7**

Common chamomile is not common at all; in fact it is a rather rare plant of grassy and heathy places in the south of England. It has a daisy-like flower and feathery leaves, but being a member of the huge and complex *compositae* family this is scarcely enough to identify it. It can be told from the very similar scentless mayweed and corn chamomile by an absence of down beneath its leaves. But its most conspicuous characteristic is its sweet apple scent, for which it was once much valued in rockeries, and even planted on lawns instead of grass.

Chamomile is still cultivated on a small scale for its flower-heads, which make a fine herbal tea. The heads are gathered when the petals just begin to turn down, and are used either fresh or dried.

Hardhead, Lesser knapweed *Centaurea nigra*   [C]   **Pl. 7**

The feathery purple petals of this common wayside plant have been used in salads. Frankly, I prefer the tricks which John Clare's village girls played with them:

> They pull the little blossom threads
> From out the knapweeds button heads
> And put the husk wi many a smile
> In their white bosoms for awhile
> Who if they guess aright the swain
> That loves sweet fancys trys to gain
> Tis said that ere its lain an hour
> Twill blossom wi a second flower
> And from her white breasts hankerchief
> Bloom as they ne'er had lost a leaf.

The Shepherd's Calendar

Fruits

A number of the fruits I have included in this section are cultivated and used commercially as well as growing in the wild. Where this is the case I have not given much space to the more common kitchen uses, which can be found in any cookery book. I have concentrated instead on how to find and gather the wild varieties, and on the more unusual, traditional recipes.

Most of the remarks I made about gathering nuts and mushrooms apply equally to fruit. Do not pick large quantities from a single bush. Always gather fresh specimens that show no signs of decay or insect damage. And with the softer fruits, try and gather them into an open basket rather than a tight paper bag. The latter will not only squash the fruit but in all probability burst, leaving you with no fruit and a dry cleaner's bill.

A product that can be made with almost all fruit is, of course, the jelly. Rather than repeat the relevant directions for every entry, I felt it would be simpler to go into some detail here. The notes below apply to all species described in the following pages, apart from ash keys.

Jellys and jams form because of a chemical reaction between a substance called pectin, present in the fruit, and sugar. The pectin (and the fruit's acids, which also play a part in the reaction) tend to be most concentrated when the fruit is under-ripe. But then of course the flavour is only partly developed. So the optimum time for picking fruit for jelly is when it is *just* ripe.

Now the amount of pectin available varies from fruit to fruit. Apples, gooseberries and currants, for instance, are rich in pectin and acid and set very readily. Blackberries and strawberries, on the other hand, have a low pectin content, and usually need to have some added from an outside source before they will form a jelly. Lemon juice or sour crab apples are commonly used for this. (There are more details about this below, and I have specified for the useful jelly-makers in this section whether they need to have pectin added.)

The first stage in making a jelly is to pulp the fruit. Do this by packing the clean fruit into a saucepan or preserving pan and *just* covering with water. Bring to the boil and simmer until all the fruit is mushy. With the harder-skinned fruits (blackcurrants, haws, etc) you may need to help the process along by pressing with a spoon, and be prepared to simmer for up to half an hour. This is the stage to supplement the pectin, if your fruit has poor setting properties. Add the juice of one lemon for every two lbs of fruit.

When you have your pulp, separate the juice from the roughage and fibres by straining through muslin. This is most easily done by lining a large bowl with a good-sized sheet of muslin, folded at least double, and filling the bowl with the fruit pulp. Then lift and tie the corners of the muslin, using the back of a chair or a low clothes line as the support, so that it hangs like a sock above the bowl. Alternatively, use a real stocking.

To obtain the maximum volume of juice, allow the pulp to strain overnight. It is not too serious to squeeze the muslin if you are in a hurry, but it will force some of the solid matter through and affect the clarity of your jelly. When you have all the juice you want, measure its volume, and transfer it to a clean saucepan with one lb of preserving sugar for every pint of juice. Bring to the boil, stirring well, and boil rapidly, skimming off any scum that floats to the surface. A jelly will normally form when the mixture has reached a temperature of 221 degrees F on a jam thermometer. If you have no thermometer, or want a confirmatory test, transfer one drop of the mixture with a spoon on to a cold saucer. If setting is imminent, the drop will not run after a few seconds because of a skin – often visible – formed across it.

As soon as the setting temperature has been achieved, pour the mixture into some clear, warm jam jars (preferably standing on a metal surface to conduct away some of the heat). Cover the surface of the jelly with a wax disc, wax side down. Add a cellophane cover, moistening it on the outside first so that it dries taut. Hold the cover in place with a rubber band, label the jar clearly, and store in a cool place.

Another process which can be applied to most of the harder-skinned fruits is drying. Choose slightly unripe fruit, wash well, and dry in a cloth. Then strew it out on a metal tray and place in a very low oven (120° F). The fruit is dry when it yields no juice when squeezed between the fingers, but is not so far gone that it rattles. This usually takes between 4 and 6 hours.

Barberry *Berberis vulgaris* [A]   **Pl. 8**

Local names: GUILD TREE, Selk; JAUNDICE TREE, Corn, Som; PIPPERIDGE, Hants, S. Eng, E. Ang, Lincs, N. Eng; WOOD-SOUR, Oxf.

Widespread but very local in hedgerows and bushy places. A spiny shrub, 6' to 10' high, with sharply toothed oval leaves and clusters of small yellow flowers. Berries from July, scarlet, oblong and in clusters.

The barberry is now a sadly diminishing shrub in our hedgerows, almost eradicated by the Black Rust fungus. Once it was a common species in hedgerows and gardens where it was cultivated for its ornamental properties, for the supposed power of its roots to cure jaundice, and for its oblong berries. These hang in brilliant red clusters, like medicinal capsules, and make one of the most pleasantly tart of jellies.

If you should find a barberry bush, you will probably need gloves and a pair of scissors to retrieve the berries, as the thorns are very fierce. They make jelly easily without additional pectin. But as you will probably only have a small quantity, try strewing them whole over roast mutton for its last few minutes in the oven, so that the berries burst and the juice runs over the meat. They are fairly sharp used in this way, but a good foil to fat meat.

The berries have also been candied, pickled and preserved in sugar for use in curries.

Raspberry *Rubus idaeus* [A]

Local names: ARNBERRY, Yks; HINDBERRY, Staff, Lancs, Yks, Cumb, N'thum, Scot; WOOD-RASP, Selk.

Widespread throughout the British Isles, and quite frequent in hedgerows, rocky woods, and heaths. A slender shrub, with usually unbranched, arching stems growing up to 6' high, and only very slightly spiny. Leaves toothed and oval, and often whitish below. Flowers small and white in drooping clusters. Fruit from July to September, a rich red berry, formed by a number of drupelets.

Although many raspberry plants growing in the wild are bird-seeded from cultivated stock, the fruit is as authentic a British native as its close relative the blackberry (see p. 163). It is not difficult to see why, of the two, it was the raspberry that was taken into gardens. It grows more tidily and with greater restraint than the spiny, aggressive bramble. And this of course means that it has been less prolific in the wild – another good reason for nurturing the plant in the non-competitive security of the garden. The berry is probably the best of all the soft fruits. Wordsworth, whose verse 'Foresight' is believed to be about the raspberry, clearly felt for it, and gave good picking advice if rather mediocre poetry;

> Hither soon as spring is fled
> You and Charles and I will walk;
> Lurking berries, ripe and red,
> Then will hang from every stalk,
> Each within its leafy bower;
> And for that promise spare the flower!

And 'as soon as spring is fled' is precisely when you will find it. It is usually the first soft fruit to ripen, occasionally as early as the last weeks of June. If you have difficulty distinguishing young raspberries from unripe blackberries, look at the stems on which they are growing. The raspberry has woody, cane-like stems, comparatively smooth except for a few weak prickles; the blackberry has much coarser stems armed with a great number of strong prickles.

The berries themselves are quite different in texture, even when they are similarly coloured. Raspberries have a matt, spongy surface, whilst blackberries are covered with a shiny, taut skin. And when fully ripe the raspberry comes away very easily from its pithy core.

Raspberries are such a rich and substantial fruit that it would be a waste to make jelly from them. But simmered in their own juice for about a quarter of an hour, and then boiled to setting point with an equal weight of sugar, they make a very fine jam.

If you only find a handful of wild berries, use them for stuffing game birds, or to make the famous summer pudding. This needs no cooking, but must be made the day before it is needed. Cut some fairly thick slices of bread and remove the crusts. Moisten them with milk, and line the sides and bottom of a deep pudding basin with them. (Make sure that the slices overlap well, so that they will hold together when turned out.) Then fill the pudding basin with a mixture of cooked raspberries, and any red, white or black currants that are available. Cover the top with more slices of moistened bread, and then with greaseproof paper. Put a weight on top of the paper and leave the pudding to stand in the refrigerator overnight. Turn out of the mould carefully and serve with cream.

Blackberry, Bramble *Rubus fruticosus* [A]

Local names for the fruit: BLACKBIDES, Kirk, Wight; BLACK BLEGS, Yks; BLACK BOWOURS, Berw; BLACK BOYDS, W. Scot; BLACK KITES, Cumb; BLACK SPICE, Yks; BLAGGS, Yks; BRAMMEL KITES, Dur; BUMBLE KITES, Hants, Yks, Cumb, N'thum; BUMMEL BERRIES, Cumb; DOCTOR'S MEDICINE, Som; GATTER-BERRY, Rox; GARTEN-BERRIES, Scot; MOOCHES, Glos; MULBERRIES, Suff, Norf; MUSHES, Dev.

Widespread and abundant in woods, hedges, waste places and heaths. A prickly shrub, usually growing in straggly, tangled clumps. The leaves are also prickly and toothed, and turn reddish-purple in the autumn. Flowers: 5 white or pinkish petals. The fruit is made up of a number of drupelets, and turns from green to red to a deep purple-black. It can be picked from August to early October.

There is little need to write at length about this juicy purple berry, which has been known, loved and picked across the world for generations. Its seeds have even been found in the stomach of a Neolithic man dug up from the Essex clay. Every September, in Europe and America, the commons and scrubland around every big town swarm with pickers, stuffing the berries into mouths and handkerchiefs and polythene bags. Blackberries have a special role in the relationship between townspeople and the countryside. It is not just that they are delicious, and easy to find. Blackberrying carries with it a little of the urban dweller's myth of country life: abundance, harvest, a sense of season, and just enough discomfort to quicken the senses. Maybe it is the scuffling and the scratches that are the real attraction of blackberrying, the proof of satisfying toil against unruly nature.

Everyone has their favourite picking habits and recipes, and these are better guides than anything a book can say. So I will confine myself here to a few of the lesser known facts about the fruit.

Blackberry bushes spread in a curious way. Each cane begins by growing erectly, but then curves downwards until its tip touches the ground. Here the shoot takes root, and a clump of new canes soon form. The berries themselves form in large clusters at the end of the older shoots, which die after two or three years' cropping. The lowest berry – right at the tip of the stalk – is the first to ripen, and is the sweetest and fattest of all. Eat it raw. A few weeks later, the other berries near the end ripen; these are less juicy, but are still good for jam and pies. The small berries farther up the stalk often do not ripen until October. They are hard and slightly bitter and are only really useful if cooked with some other fruit.

There are any number of recipes which make use of blackberries. They can be made into pies and summer puddings (see raspberries), fruit fools and salads, jellies (they need a little extra pectin), and jams. A good way of serving them fresh is to leave them to steep overnight in red wine.

The most delicious blackberry product I know is a junket made from nothing other than blackberry juice. Remove the juice from the very ripest berries with the help of a juice extractor, or by pressing them through several layers of muslin. Then simply allow the thick, dark juice to stand undisturbed in a warm room. Do not stir or cool the juice, or add anything to it. In a few hours it will have set to the consistency of a light junket, and can be eaten with cream and sweet biscuits.

Dewberry *Rubus caesius* [B]

Widespread and frequent in bushy and grassy places, especially in Eastern England.

The dewberry carries a smaller fruit than the blackberry, with fewer segments, and covered with a fine bloom. In all other respects, though, it can be looked on as a blackberry.

Wild strawberry *Fragaria vesca* [A]

Widespread and common on grassy banks, heaths, open woods. A low, creeping plant with hairy runners and stalks. The leaves are in groups of three, toothed, shiny green above, and silky grey beneath. Fruits, late June to August, small drooping red berries with the seeds protruding.

The tiny fruits of the wild strawberry are often no bigger than a child's beads. Yet each one holds more sweetness and flavour than any of the monsters grown for commerce. Most of these are freaks, so dogmatically bred to astonish by their colour and size that their insides taste like snow.

It was one of the American wood strawberries, *Fragaria virginiana*, which was the origin of most of the large-fruited varieties we cultivate today. It was probably introduced to Europe soon after 1600. Before this, strawberries found in gardens were simply wild plants which had been transplanted from the woods in the early spring. Sheltered and manured, they fruit more plentifully than in the wild, but never show much improvement in size.

In some parts of the country wild strawberries are abundant, and carpet wide patches of dry and heathy ground. But normally you will need to search carefully for them, looking for the trefoil leaves in the bracken edges and rough grass. The drooping berries can be even more elusive and are often completely hidden by the leaves. To add to the confusion, there will doubtless be barren strawberry plants mixed in. These are very similar to wild strawberries and grow in the same habitats, but bear fruits quite unlike the strawberry, and have smaller and less shiny leaves.

Wild strawberries are so succulent that they are best eaten fresh, with cream. They need very little sugar. They also make good jam, with the addition of a small amount of lemon juice, and a filling for tarts.

Rose-hip *Rosa canina*   [A]   **Pl. 8**

(For details of the wild rose, see p. 151.)
Local names for the fruit: BUCKIE BERRIES, N. Ire; CANKERS,
Dor, Ess, Norf, Cam; CHOOPS, Yks, Dur, Cumb, Rox, Dumf,
Ayr; DOG-JOBS, Yks; HAGISSES, Hants; HAWS, Dor; HEDGE-
SPEAKS, Glos; HEDGE-PEDGIES, Wilts; HIPSONS, Oxf;
HUGGANS, Yks; ITCHING-BERRIES, Lancs; NIPPERNAILS,
Ches; PIG'S NOSES, Dev; PIXIE PEARS, Dev, Hants; SOLDIERS,
Kent.

The fruit is an orange-red, oblong berry, sometimes as much as
an inch long, and is on the bushes between late August and
November.

The fruit of the wild rose, the hip, is the star of the one great
success story of wild food use. It is the only completely wild fruit
which supports a national commercial enterprise – the production
of rose-hip syrup. There are no roses under cultivation to
supplement the wild hips; nor, to my knowledge, do the
manufacturers employ any professional pickers.

It was not until the war, when our supplies of citrus fruits were
virtually cut off, that the potentialities of rose-hips as a source of
Vitamin C were taken seriously. But the fruit had been used as a
food for centuries before that. When cultivated fruit was scarce in
the Middle Ages, rose-hips were used as a dessert. Gerard speaks
highly of the fruit: 'When it is ripe, the fruit maketh the most
pleasant meates and banketting dishes or tartes'. A recipe from
1730 explains how this hard, unlikely berry was transformed into
a filling for tarts. The hips were first slit in half, and the pith and
seeds thoroughly cleaned out. Then the skins were put to stand in
an earthenware pot until they were soft enough to rub through a
sieve. (Notice that this was done without the use of any heat or
liquid.) The resulting purée was mixed with its own weight of
sugar, warmed until the sugar melted, and then potted.

During the First World War it was suggested that British
housewives should make jam from rose-hips. But their patience
was understandably less then than it had been in Gerard's day, and
the labour of cleaning out each hip individually was a fairly
effective deterrent. Yet this is essential if the flesh of the hips is
to be used, as it would be in a jam. The seeds of the hip are

covered with stiff, sharply pointed hairs, and if any of these are left adhering to the skins in a preserve they can become a dangerous internal irritant, especially to children.

Then, in 1934, it was discovered that the fruits of English wild roses contained more Vitamin C than any other fruit or vegetable, four times as much as blackcurrants in fact, and twenty times as much as oranges.

But it was not until the Second World War began to seriously disrupt our usual sources of Vitamin C that the government began to consider the use of Rose-hips. In 1941 the Ministry of Health put forward a scheme for collection, and in that year 120 tons were gathered by voluntary collectors. The next year the scheme was transferred to the Vegetable Drugs Committee of the Ministry of Supply and 344 tons were gathered. By 1943 the redoubtable County Herb Committees (see introduction) were brought in to organise the collection, and for the next three years the harvest averaged 450 tons.

During these war years all this fruit was converted into rose-hip syrup by commercial manufacturers. Under-ripe berries were preferred, in case of transport hold-ups, and were dispatched from local centres direct to the factories. Here they were put through an elaborate process designed to produce syrup with the minimum destruction of Vitamin C. The hips were leached with boiling water immediately after grinding, to destroy an enzyme which inactivates the Vitamin C very rapidly. Whilst the hips remain whole this enzyme is unable to attack the vitamin; but as soon as the cell walls are broken it is liberated. Further conservation measures were taken during the extraction and concentration of the juices, which was done under reduced pressure to avoid the need for excessive heat.

The resulting syrup was sold through ordinary retailers at a controlled price of 1s 9d a six ounce bottle. Mothers and children were able to obtain it in larger quantities, and at reduced prices, from Welfare Clinics.

The story continues. Rose-hip syrup is still produced commercially, and the manufacturers still rely on voluntary collectors. Most of these are schoolchildren, and the 2 or 3p per lb they receive for the fruit is apparently quite an incentive, for prodigious quantities are collected in some areas, particularly the North. An average primary school would expect to gather about 1000 lbs in a normal winter. But one Carlisle secondary school exceeded 30,000 lbs during the record winter of 1964.

One upland village school based an enterprising project around rose-hips as part of their participation in the Nuffield Junior Science Project. They were persuaded to forfeit some of their income and bring their weekend's pickings into class. Amidst some more respectable scientific experimentation a great deal of syrup was made by boiling the topped and tailed hips all day in the school canteen! This apparent contempt for the vitamin content appeared to have little serious affect, for when the children proudly sent a sample of their syrup to the local Public Analyst, he reported that it contained 65 mg of Vitamin C per fluid ounce. As commercial syrup normally aims at 70 mg per fluid ounce, one wonders if that elaborate wartime process was not over-cautious.

The children also sent a questionnaire to the commercial producers of the syrup. The answers they received were rather evasive, and to the question 'What other products can be produced from rose-hips besides syrup' the manufacturers replied with a terse 'none'. One of the children, indignant at this attitude, promptly invented rose-hip lollies. Another, as a bonus, re-discovered the power of rose-hip seeds as an itching powder.

But the syrup is really the beginning of all useful rose-hip recipes, and making it is the simplest way of filtering out those ferocious prickles. Here, as a nostalgic but highly functional guide, are the meticulous directions given by the Ministry of Food during the war:

Have ready 3 pints of boiling water, mince the hips in a coarse mincer, drop immediately into the boiling water or if possible mince the hips directly into the boiling water and again bring to the boil. Stop heating and place aside for 15 minutes. Pour into a flannel or linen crash jelly bag and allow to drip until the bulk of the liquid has come through. Return the residue to the saucepan, add 1½ pints of boiling water, stir and allow to stand for 10 minutes. Pour back into the jelly bag and allow to drip. To make sure all the sharp hairs are removed put back the first half cupful of liquid and allow to drip through again. Put the mixed juice into a clean saucepan and boil down until the juice measures about 1½ pints, then add 1¼ lbs of sugar and boil for a further 5 minutes. Pour into hot sterile bottles and seal at once. If corks are used these should have been boiled for ¼ hour just previously and after insertion coated with melted paraffin wax. It is advisable to use small bottles as the syrup will not keep for more than a week or two once the bottle is opened. Store in a dark cupboard.

Hedgerow Harvest, MoF, 1943

The resulting syrup can be used as a flavouring for milk puddings, ice-cream or almost any sweet, or diluted as a drink.

Sloe, Blackthorn *Prunus spinosa* [A] Pl. 8

Local names for the fruit: BULLENS, Shrop; HEG-PEGS, Glos; HEDGE-PICKS, Hants; HEDGE-SPEAKS, Wilts; SLAGS, Oxf; SNAGS, Dor, Som, Wilts, Hants; WINTER KECKSIES, IoW; WINTER PICKS, Suss.

Widespread and abundant in woods and hedgerows throughout the British Isles, though thinning out in the north of Scotland. A stiff, dense shrub, up to 12' high, with long thorns and oval leaves. The flowers are small and pure white and appear before the leaves. Fruit: a small, round, very dark-blue berry covered when young with a paler bloom.

The sloe is the ancestor of all our cultivated plums. Crossed with the cherry-plum (*Prunus cerasifera*, p. 170), selected, crossed again, it eventually produced fruits as sweet and sumptuous as the Victoria. Yet the wild sloe is the tartest, most acid berry you will ever taste. Just one cautious bite into the green flesh will make the whole of the inside of your mouth creep. But a barrowload of sloe-stones were collected during the excavation of a Neolithic lake village at Glastonbury. Were they just used for dyeing? Or did our ancestors have hardier palates than us?

But for all its potent acidity, the sloe is very far from being a useless fruit. It makes a clear, sprightly jelly, and that most agreeable of liqueurs, sloe gin.

The best time to pick sloes for this drink is immediately after the first frost, which makes the skins softer and more permeable. Sloe gin made at this time will, providentially, just be ready in time for Christmas. Pick about a pound of the marble-sized berries (you will probably need a glove as the spines are stiff and sharp). If they have not been through a frost, pierce the skins of each one with a skewer, to help the gin and the juices get together more easily. Mix the sloes with an equal weight of sugar, and half fill the bottles with this mixture. Pour gin into the bottles until they are nearly full, and seal tightly. Store for at least two months, and shake occasionally to help dissolve and disperse the sugar. The result is a brilliant, deep pink liqueur, sour-sweet and refreshing to taste, and demonstrably potent. Don't forget to eat the berries from the bottle, which will have quite lost their bitter edge, and soaked up a fair amount of the gin themselves.

There are a number of other *Prunus* (plums and cherries) species growing wild in Britain. They fruit unpredictably and irregularly, and what they do produce is often so bitter that it can only be used, like the sloe, in liqueurs and jellies (the cherries may need a little extra pectin).

Cherry-plum *Prunus cerasifera*　[B]

Locally common in hedgerows in a few scattered areas in England. The twigs are brown, not dark-grey like blackthorn, and without thorns. The fruits appear rather earlier than sloes and are reddish-yellow in colour.

This is not a cross between a cherry and a plum, but a distinct species, and is one of the two ancestors of the domestic plum. It often does not produce any fruit, but what does appear can be used cooked if well sweetened.

Bullace *Prunus domestica*　[B]

Occurs occasionally in hedgerows throughout the British Isles. Fruits like large, egg-shaped sloes, though of variable colours.

The bullace was the domestic plum before cultivation produced the more succulent varieties. Its fruit is not quite as sour as the sloe, but is still normally left on the branch until the early frosts have reduced some of its acidity.

Wild cherry *Prunus avium* [B]

Widespread and frequent in hedgerows and woods, especially beech. A lofty tree with shining, reddish-brown bark and an abundance of white flowers in the spring. The fruit is like a small, dark-red, cultivated cherry.

The fruit of the wild cherry can be either sweet or bitter. It used to be sold occasionally in London on the branch.

Morello cherry *Prunus cerasus* [B]

Rare, in hedges and woods on acid soils. A much smaller shrub than the wild cherry, with a dark, bitter fruit.

Used commercially for making liqueurs.

Bird cherry *Prunus padus* [B]

Quite frequent in woods and hedgerows, mainly in the north of England. Told from the last two species by its long spikes of smaller flowers, and its bitter, black, pea-sized fruit.

Hawthorn *Crataegus monogyna* [A]

(See p. 82 for details of the hawthorn bush.)
Local names for berries: numerous, including HAWS (most common); AGALD, AGARVE, AGASSE, AGGLE, AGOG, BIRD'S EGGLE, BIRD'S MEAT, CHAW, CUCKOO'S BEADS, HAG, HALVE, HARVE, HIPPERTYHAW, HAZLE, HEETHEN-BERRY, HEGPEG, HOGAIL, HOGARVE, HOGGAN, HOGGOSSE, MAY-FRUIT, PIG-ALL, PIG-BERRY, PIXY-PEAR.

Haws are perhaps the most abundant berry of all in the autumn. Almost every hawthorn bush is festooned with small bunches of the round, dark-red berries, looking a little like spherical hips. They make a moderate jelly, but being a dry fruit need long simmering with a few crab apples to bring out all the juices and provide the necessary pectin. Otherwise the jelly will be sticky or rubbery. It is a good accompaniment to cream cheese.

171

Personally I prefer haws eaten straight off the bush. Their creamy flesh, stripped off the central stone, is not unlike sweet potato.

Rowan, Mountain ash *Sorbus aucuparia* [A]   **Pl. 8**

Local names for fruit: CARES, Corn, Dev; COCK-DRUNKS, Cumb; DOG-BERRIES, Ches, Cumb, Lakes; POISON-BERRIES, Som, Yks, N'thum; QUICKEN-BERRIES, Ire.

Widespread and common in dry woods and rocky places, especially in the north and west of the British Isles. A small tree with fairly smooth grey bark, toothed leaves, grouped in alternate pairs and umbels of small white flowers. Fruit: large clusters of small orange berries, August to November.

The rowan is a favourite municipal tree, and is planted in great numbers along the edges of residential highways, where urban thrushes feast off its berries. You will not be popular if you start cropping them as well, but you should not have too much trouble in finding wild rowan trees. Their clusters of brilliant orange fruits are unmistakeable in almost every setting, against grey limestone in the uplands, or the deep evergreens of Scots pine on wintery heaths. Unless the birds have got there first, rowan berries can hang on the trees until January. They are best picked in October, when they have their full colour but have not yet become mushy.

You should cut the clusters whole from the trees, trim off any excess stalk, and then make a jelly in the usual way, with the addition of a little chopped crab apple to provide the pectin. (You should be able to find crabs growing not far away from your rowans.)

The jelly is a deliciously dark orange, with a sharp, marmaladish flavour, and is perfect with game and lamb.

Crab apple *Malus sylvestris* [A]

Local names: SCRAB, N. Eng, N'thum, Scot; BITTERSGALL, Som; GRIBBLE, Dor, Som; GRINDSTONE APPLE, Wilts;

SCROGG, Dur, N'thum, Berw, Rox; SOUR GRABS, Som; WILDING-TREE, Shrop.

Widespread and frequent in woods, hedgerows and heaths. A small tree, with reddish-brown twigs and spines when truly wild. Leaves: oval, toothed and usually downy. The apples are round, yellowish green (sometimes turning scarlet) and can be picked from July to December.

How often one was lectured as a child on the dangers of eating crab apples. Worms, stomach cramps and all manner of unpleasant consequences were promised as deterrents. Yet how tempting the crabs looked in autumn, hanging there neat and child's pocket-sized, in all shades of green and yellow and red.

It is lucky that early man was easily tempted, and had no over-protective parents to hold him back, or we would be without the most famous fruit in the world.

Wild crab apples are the origin of all our manifold cultivated species, and have been used as food since antiquity. The pips are often found embedded in remnants of prehistoric cooking pots. The American Indians used to bury the crabs in the autumn and dig them up again in the spring, by which time they had lost much of their bitterness.

You may come across crab apple trees in almost any situation, but they do like light, and the best fruiters will be in dense hedges and heaths. The fruit itself can show some variation in size and colour. Not only is the wild apple a variable species in its own right, but large numbers of domestic apples have seeded themselves in the wild, and either reverted to a wild form or crossed with true crabs. There are over 3,000 named varieties of apples in cultivation, representing an enormous bank of genetic variation. Yet drop a selection of cores in the wild, and the seedlings that survive will all bear fruit not much different from the range of crab apples. There is no place in a competitive environment for the fancy colourings and fleshy shells that we have teased from the much less pronounced variations in the wild stock.

But most hedgerow crabs probably have a domestic apple somewhere amongst their ancestors, and this helps to increase the variety of the wild stock. The closer they are to their domestic

173

parents, the larger and sweeter their fruit will be. I have often found wild apples which are perfectly edible raw, though admittedly sharp.

But the true European crab (and varieties like *Malus baccata*, the East Asian species commonly planted in parks for its brilliant red, cherry-like fruits) are normally unpalatable raw. Yet the uses which they can be put to in the kitchen are enormous. They make one of the best jellies of all wild fruits – deep-pink to yellow-green, depending on the colour of your crop. Allowed to ferment they make cider, or that precursor of vinegar, verjuice. This is really a very sharp cider, and for making pickles it was often distilled. To make verjuice, take some ripe crabs and lay in a heap until they begin to sweat. Remove the stalks and the really rotten fruit, beat the remainder to a mash in a large bowl, and press through a coarse cloth (or juice extractor). Bottle the verjuice, which will be ready for use in a month's time.

But the great crab apple recipe is certainly lambs wool, a cheerful and warming drink of great antiquity made from hot ale, spices and crab apples. This is the drink Shakespeare is referring to when he talks of roasted crabs hissing in the bowl (*Love's Labours Lost*). Puck, too, mentions the drink:

> And sometimes lurk I in a gossip's bowl,
> In very likeness of a roasted crab,
> And when she drinks, against her lips I bob.
>
> (*Midsummer Night's Dream*)

Erik Linklater has some of the characters in his novel *Poet's Pub* drinking lamb's wool before a gargantuan Elizabethan feast, and I don't know of any more useful or evocative recipe:

Saturday and Joan returned with a bowl that perfumed the room and made all mouths water with its rich October smell. Lamb's wool is a mixture of hot ale, the pulp of roasted apples, a little sugar, and a little spice. Much depends on the quality of the apples; more on the ale. Saturday had discovered that even the best apples and the oldest ale are improved by an egg or two beaten up in thin cream with enough whisky to counteract the fatness of the cream. His lamb's wool was drunk in silence, the silence of appreciation, the quietness of content.

Poet's Pub

Red currant *Ribes rubrum* [A]

Local names: GAZEL, Kent; RIZZLES, Kirk, Wigt; WINEBERRY, Yks, Cumb, Lakes, Scot.

Widespread but local in woods and hedgerows, especially by streams and fens. A bush, 2′ to 4′ high, with toothed leaves broken into 3 or 5 lobes. Flowers: small, green and drooping. Fruits from July, round and shiny red, with a slightly translucent skin.

This familiar shrub is almost certainly a native, but many of the plants found in the wild are blatant escapes from nearby gardens. Nevertheless, it is not uncommon by the sides of rivers and streams, especially in rough fenland. Beware of confusion with the very similar guelder rose. This is also a waterside shrub with lobed leaves and red fruit. But the berries lack a 'tail' and look heavy and waxy beside the bright, translucent skins of the red currant.

Red currants contain an obtrusive number of pips, and a jelly is probably the best way of making use of them. There is no need to add extra pectin.

(See p. 181 for notes on the closely related black currant.)

Gooseberry *Ribes uva-crispa* [A]

Local names: CARBERRY, Yks, N. Eng; CATBERRY, West, Cumb; DAYBERRY, Corn, Dev, Kent; FEABERRY, S. Eng, E. Ang, War, Shrop, Ches, Derb, Leic, Lancs, Yks; GOGGLE, Lincs; GOLFOB, Derb; GOOSEGOG, Som, Hants, Herts, Middx, E. Ang, N'thants, Ches, Lincs, Yks; GROSET, Scot; GROSSBERRY, Yks; GROZZLE, Rox, Dumf; HONEY-BLOB, Scot; WINEBERRY, Yks.

Widespread and not infrequent in woods and hedgerows. A stubby, many branched shrub, rarely growing more than 3′ high, with 3- or 4-lobed, blunt-toothed leaves, and drooping, red-tinged, green flowers. Fruit: greenish yellow, egg-shaped and usually hairy. July onwards.

Like the other members of the *Ribes* family, gooseberries were

175

late coming into cultivation, presumably because the wild fruit was quite satisfactory in its own right.

In some areas of the north, the hedges can be thick with gooseberries, and with the help of a pair of gloves you should be able to pick a fair quantity.

Depending on their ripeness and sweetness they can be used in any of the recipes which normally employ the cultivated fruit. The ripe berries make gooseberry pie or gooseberry fool, the under-ripe ones gooseberry jelly. (See the recipe with elder flowers on p. 155.)

One of the classic recipes for gooseberry is a sauce for serving with mackerel. Top and tail about half a pound of berries, and stew in as little water as possible until they are soft and pulped. Beat well, and then put through a sieve or purée in a blender. Mix in 1 oz of butter, and a little sugar if the fruit is sour.

Gervase Markham gives a marvellously excessive recipe for gooseberry tansy:

Put some fresh butter in a frying pan; when it is melted put into it a quart of gooseberries, fry them till they are tender and break them all to a mash; then beat seven eggs, but four whites, a pound of sugar, three spoonfuls of sack, much cream, a penny loaf grated, and three spoonfuls of flour; mix all these together, then put the gooseberries out of the pan to them, and stir well together, and put them into a saucepan to thicken, then put butter into the frying pan and fry them brown.

The English Hus-Wife

With some juggling of quantities and the omission of the 'much cream' this recipe ought still to produce very acceptable results.

Bilberry *Vaccinium myrtillus* [A]

Local names: WHORTLEBERRY. ARTS, Som, Wilts; BLACK-BERRY, Yks; BLAEBERRY, Shrop, Lancs, Yks, West, Cumb, N'thum, Scot, Ire; BLUEBERRY, Yks, Cumb, Ire; BRYLOCKS, Scot; COWBERRY, Som; CROWBERRY, Mor; HARTBERRY, Dor, Som; HURTLEBERRY, Dev, Som; HURTS, Corn, Dev, Som, Hants, Glos, Suss, Surr, Pemb; WHORTS, Corn, Dev, Som,

Hants, Suss, Surr; WIMBERRY, Glos, Heref, Shrop, Ches, Derb, Lancs, N. Eng.

Widespread throughout the British Isles, except the south and east of England, and locally abundant on heaths and moors. An erect undershrub, growing 9″ to 18″ high, with hairless twigs and oval, slightly toothed, bright green leaves. Flowers: solitary, drooping, greenish-pink globes. Fruits from July to September, small, round and black.

The bilberry is an intriguingly juicy and versatile fruit, and would doubtless be more popular commercially if picking it were not such a laborious business. The shrub grows low, often largely concealed by dense heather, and the berries form in nothing like the concentrations of, say, blackberries. So even on the moors where the bush grows in abundance, gathering any quantity can involve the thorough scouring of a fair-sized patch of land.

The fruit is a little acid when raw, but can be eaten fresh with cream and sugar. Cooked, it can take its place in almost any fruit recipe; crumbles, pancakes and fruit stews. The bilberry is very succulent and rarely needs much extra liquid added during cooking. The jelly and jam need none at all (though lemon juice is needed for the set). Nor does that American national dish, bilberry pie, which is simply the fresh berries, sprinkled with sugar and lemon juice, baked inside a double crust pie.

The American Indians dried the fruit and used it for flavouring soups and stews.

Elder *Sambucus nigra* [A]

(For details see p. 154.)

Fruits, August to October, clusters of small, reddish-black berries.

I have seen elder bushes so laden with fruit that the top boughs were bent down nearly to ground level. The fruits are relished by birds, but rarely by humans, perhaps because of their rather cloying taste when raw. But they are useful as additions to a number of cooked recipes in which any unpleasant aftertaste completely disappears.

The berries are ripe when the clusters begin to turn upside

F.F.—M

down. Gather the clusters whole by cutting them from the stems, picking only those where the very liquid berries have not started to wrinkle or melt. Wash them well, and strip them from the stalks with a fork. They are good added whole to apple pies, or added as a make-weight to blackberry jelly. (Both berries are on the bush at the same time, so if you are making this they can be gathered straight into the same basket.)

My favourite elderberry recipe is for Pontack Sauce, a relic from those days when every retired military gentleman carried his patent sauce as an indispensable part of his luggage. Pontack's was a famous restaurant in Lombard Street which was no doubt on these gentlemen's town circuit, and from there this recipe was taken back to the country seats and adjusted to the owner's idiosyncrasies. There are any number of variants of Pontack Sauce, particularly from the hunting country in the Midlands. This one from Leicestershire probably used claret instead of vinegar in the original (Pontack's was owned by Château Haut Brion).

Pour one pint of boiling vinegar (or claret) over one pint of elderberries in a stone jar or casserole dish. Cover, and allow the jar to stand overnight in an oven at very low heat. Next day pour off the liquid, put it in a saucepan with a teaspoon of salt, a blade of mace, 40 peppercorns, 12 cloves, a finely chopped onion and a little ginger. Boil for ten minutes and then bottle securely with the spices.

The sauce was reputedly meant to be kept for seven years before use. My patience ran out after seven days, but having made rather a large bottle, I can report a distinct improvement in richness after the first year! It has a fine fruity taste, a little like a thick punch, and is especially good with liver.

Oregon grape *Mahonia aquifolium* [c]   Pl. 8

A member of the barberry family, and now more plentiful than the common barberry itself. It is an evergreen shrub, up to four feet high, and infrequent but widespread in the south. Many specimens are naturalised from shrubberies and game coverts. The berries are majestically dark, white-bloomed, and hang in bunches, like miniature grapes. They can be eaten raw or made into jelly.

Hottentot fig *Caprobrotus edulis* [C]   **Pl. 8**

This garden plant from South Africa – better known by its old name of *Mesembyanthemum* – is now naturalised in the warm climate of Devon and Cornwall. There, near the sea, its matted, succulent foliage and silky pink flowers can breathe a hint of the tropics into the most stolid British cliff.

Its fruits, the figs, are edible and pleasantly tangy.

Cloudberry *Rubus chamaemorus* [C]   **Pl. 8**

This little shrub, which grows not much more than six inches high, is a relative of the blackberry. It grows in patches on the damp heather moors of Scotland and the north of England. In autumn, the hard berries turn a delicate marmalade orange. They are often used, in northern counties, for puddings or jams, or indeed any dish that is conventionally made from blackberries or raspberries.

Medlar *Mespilus germanica* [C]   **Pl. 8**

The curious fact about the medlar is that its fruits need to be half-rotten – or 'bletted' – before they are edible. This seems to be a result of our climate not being warm enough to ripen the fruits, for in Mediterranean regions, where the tree is more widespread, the young fruit can be eaten straight off the tree. Here it stays rock-hard until mid-winter.

The whole tree is something of a curiosity. It is probably a native, but only occurs very occasionally in hedgerows in the South, usually in gnarled, eccentric shapes produced by the wood's sensitivity to the wind. The fruit is strange to look at, like a giant brown rose-hip, with the five-tailed calyx protruding from the head of the fruit like a crown.

When the fruits are fully bletted, the brown flesh can be scraped out of the skin and eaten with cream and sugar. Or the fruits can be baked whole, like apples, or made into jelly.

June berry *Amelanchier intermedia* [C]

A rare shrub naturalised in woodlands in a few areas of the south of England. The purplish-red berries are sweet to taste, and can be eaten uncooked, or made into pies. In America they are sometimes canned for winter use.

Whitebeam *Sorbus aria* [C]   **Pl. 8**

A very striking shrub, flashed with silver when the wind turns up the pale undersides of the leaves. The bunched red berries are edible as soon as they begin to 'blet' – or go rotten, like medlars. John Evelyn found them 'not unpleasant', and recommended them in a concoction with new wine and honey.

Whitebeam is locally frequent in scrub and copses in the south of England, and is popular as a suburban roadside tree.

French hales *Sorbus latifolia* [C]

French Hales is a close relative of whitebeam. It still grows locally in some of the old woods in the south-west of England, though it is practically unknown elsewhere. In Devon the brown fruits have been sold and eaten.

Wild service tree *Sorbus torminalis* [C]

In the nineteenth century, the fruits of the wild service tree were sold in the markets of the south of England under the unlikely name of Chequers. The chief buyers were apparently children whose taste for the bizarre in food no doubt relished these diminutive fruits: like other *sorbus* species, they are only edible when half rotten.

The fruit resembles a cross between a rowan berry and a crab apple, and is forbiddingly acid to boot. The shrub is rare in Britain, and occurs only locally in woods in the south.

Pear *Pyrus communis* [C]

Pyrus communis is the ancestor of all our cultivated pears. It is a handsome tree which grows wild all over Europe, and the varieties we eat today began to be developed less than 200 years ago in France and Belgium.

In Britain it is scarcely distributed in woods and hedgerows in the south of England; and even here the wildness of some specimens is dubious. But you can still discover the odd tree

which in October bears the tough green fruit of the true wild pear –
almost impossible to eat raw, but good enough for an astringent
jelly.

Black currant *Ribes nigrum*   [c]

The soothing properties of black currant juice were probably
known long before the plant passed into cultivation, for it was
often given against sore throats and 'the quinsy'. It is a rather
uncommon plant in the wild, and can readily be told from red
currant by its larger, heavily aromatic leaves. A few of these,
dried, can transform a pot of Indian tea.

The currants can also be dried, and in this form they are one of
the bases of pemmican, an Amerindian dish taken up by Polar
explorers. The currants are pounded together with dried meat,
and the mixture bound together and coated with fat or tallow.
The result was a food containing almost all the ingredients
necessary for a balanced diet, which would keep well even on
long journeys.

Dwarf cornel *Chamaepericlymenum suecicum*   [c]

The one aperitif in this book. The small scarlet berries used to be
munched by the Highlanders to stimulate their appetites. In
America they have been eaten by the Indians, and occasionally
made into puddings.

Dwarf cornel is rare, and there are more agreeable ways to perk
up your appetite, so this tiny plant is probably best left unpicked.
Only in a few areas in the Highlands does it still thrive under the
shelter of heather and bilberry.

Strawberry-tree *Arbutus unedo*   [c]   **Pl. 8**

A small evergreen shrub from the Mediterranean, which just ekes
out a living in rocky woods in the SW tip of Ireland. The fruit is
a beguiling red berry, $\frac{3}{4}''$ across and very warty; but bite it and
your feelings may be stronger than Gerard's, who tactfully
described its taste as 'somewhat harsh'. In France, it is used in
making sweets and liqueurs.

Cranberry *Vaccinium oxycoccus* [c]

Cranberry sounds as American as that other well-known fruit dish. In fact, the origins, name and traditional uses are solidly British, and the fruit is mentioned (as 'fenberry') in a herbal published in 1578. Like so much else, cranberry recipes were preserved by British settlers in America, and only later brought back into use here.

Cranberries were once common in Britain. But the draining of much of our marsh and bogland has robbed the plant of its natural wet habitats, and it is now largely confined to the north of England and Wales. The berry of the wild plant, mottled red and $\frac{1}{4}''$ across, is inedible raw, but makes as good a sauce as the larger American variety. And it can be kept throughout the winter without decaying.

Cowberry *Vaccinium vitis-idaea* [c]

This little shrub is a close relative of the cranberry, and one of its names is in fact Mountain Cranberry. It grows to a maximum height of 12″ on some moors in the northern parts of the British Isles. Like cranberries, the red, spherical berries are sharp and scarcely edible when raw, though they make an excellent jelly. (They need some apple added for the pectin.)

Wintergreen *Pyrola minor* [c]

(See p. 87.)

Crowberry *Empetrum nigrum* [c]

The black fruits of this little creeping shrub are poor eating, but they are used in Arctic regions, and probably have some value as a source of vitamin C. In Britain the plant trails like heather over some of the northern moors.

Ash *Fraxinus excelsior* [c]

Ash keys, the single-winged fruits of the ash which hang in bundles from the tree from July onwards, have been made into a pickle. John Evelyn recommends boiling the young, green keys, changing the water, boiling again, and then pickling under hot spiced vinegar. I personally find them rather tough and bitter, but if you pick the very youngest keys you may be luckier.

Snowberry *Symphoricarpos rivularis* [c]   **Pl. 8**

The round white berries of the snowberry, like mint gobstoppers, are a familiar sight in many shrubberies. But the bush also grows wild, cropping up as a casual in hedges and copses throughout the British Isles.

The pallor of the berries makes them seem quite wrong as a food, and I can find no record of their being used in this country. Yet neither is there any record of their being harmful in any way, and I find their ethereal taste rather pleasing. Snowberries may be one of our underexploited fruits, and I would welcome the results of readers' cautious experiments.

Guelder rose *Viburnum opulus* [c]   **Pl. 8**

The sticky red fruits of the guelder rose will make you sick if you eat them raw, but they are quite safe cooked, and have often been made into jellies. In America they are sometimes used as a substitute for cranberries in sauces.

The guelder rose is a handsome shrub. It has maple-shaped leaves (see red currant p. 175) which in autumn turn a flaming crimson that almost matches the colour of the berries.

Juniper *Juniperus communis* [c]

Renowned for flavouring gin, the crushed berries also go splendidly with veal. The fruits have a curious life story lasting nearly two full years. They begin as a small berry-like cone, green in colour, and only turn black in their second year – which is when they are picked. At this stage they are rich in oil, which is the source of their value as a flavouring.

Sadly, this graceful evergreen shrub is decreasing everywhere. Since myxomatosis decimated the rabbit population, there has been little to check the growth of scrub in those habitats where the juniper flourished. It has consequently been choked out in many places by the hardier hawthorns and elders, and is now only widespread in the moors and pine woods of Scotland.

Appendix: Poisonous Plants

Below is a full list of those British plants generally regarded as poisonous to humans when eaten in moderate amounts. There are some others which it is not wise to eat because they can be damaging in large quantities. For instance, scarlet pimpernel and bracken. Both of these have been eaten safely in the past, but the former can cause anaemia, and the latter contains small quantities of a carcinogen. I have not listed such plants here, but neither are they in the text, unless a warning about the eating of large quantities accompanies them.

Fungi

Gyomitra esculenta
Ergot – *Claviceps purpurea*
Ramaria formosa
Clitocybe rivulosa
Clitocybe dealbata
Fly agaric – *Amanita muscaria*
Death cap – *Amanita phalloides*
Panther cap – *Amanita pantherina*
Lepiota cristata
Lepiota fuscovinacea
Yellow-stainer – *Agaricus xanthodermus*
Agaricus placomyces
Stropharia hornemannii
Inocybe lacera
Inocybe geophylla

Inocybe griseo-lilacina
Inocybe praetervisa
Inocybe squamata
Inocybe fastigiata
Inocybe langei
Inocybe patouillardii
Inocybe jurana
Inocybe maculata
Inocybe napipes
Inocybe asterospora
Hebeloma crustuliniforme
Rhodophyllus sinuatus
Boletus satanas
Russula emetica (when raw)
Common earth ball – *Scleroderma aurantium*

Flowering Plants (it is best to assume that all parts of the following plants are unsafe)

Stinking hellebore – *Helleborus foetidus*
Green hellebore – *Helleborus viridis*
Columbine – *Aquilegia vulgaris*
Spindle-tree – *Euonymus europaeus*

Monkshood – *Aconitum anglicum*
Baneberry – *Actaea spicata*
All species of buttercup (*Ranunculus*)
All spurges (*Euphorbia*)
Privet – *Ligustrum vulgare*

Alder buckthorn – *Frangula alnus*
Common buckthorn – *Rhamnus cathartica*
Mezereon – *Daphne mezereum*
Spurge-laurel – *Daphne laureola*
Mistletoe – *Viscum album*
Ivy – *Hedera helix*
Hemlock – *Conium maculatum*
Cowbane – *Cicuta virosa*
Tubular water dropwort – *Oenanthe fistulosa*
Hemlock water dropwort – *Oenanthe crocata*
Fine-leaved water dropwort – *Oenanthe aquatica*
Fool's parsley – *Aethusa cynapium*
White bryony – *Bryonia dioica*
Dog's mercury – *Mercurialis perennis*

Deadly nightshade – *Atropa bella-donna*
Henbane – *Hyoscyamus niger*
Bittersweet – *Solanum dulcamara*
Black nightshade – *Solanum nigrum*
Thorn-apple – *Datura stramonium*
Foxglove – *Digitalis purpurea*
Lily of the valley – *Convallaria majalis*
Fritillary – *Fritillaria meleagris*
Meadow saffron – *Colchicum autumnale*
Black bryony – *Tamus communis*
Darnel rye-grass – *Lolium temulentum*
Yew – *Taxus baccata*

Sources, References and Further Reading

ABEHSERA, Michel, *Zen Macrobiotic Cooking*, Albyn Press, 1969

AUSTIN, Thomas (ed), *Two Fifteenth Century Cook Books*, Early English Text Society, 1888

BARRETT, John, and YONGE, C. M., *Pocket Guide to the Sea Shore*, Collins, 1958

BOTANICAL SOCIETY OF THE BRITISH ISLES, *Atlas of the British Flora*, Nelson, 1962

BULLOCK, MCCULLY, NODERER, *The American Heritage Cookbook*, Penguin, 1967

BURKILL, I. H., 'Habits of Man, and the Origins of Cultivated Plants in the Old World', *Proceedings of the Linnean Society*, 164. London 1953

CALDER, Angus, *The People's War*, Jonathan Cape, 1969

CANDOLLE, A. de, *Origine des Plantes Cultives*, Paris, 1883

CHAPMAN, V. J., *Seaweeds and their Uses*, Methuen, 2nd edition 1970

CLARE, John, *The Shepherd's Calendar*, edited by Eric Robinson and Geoffrey Summerfield, Oxford 1964

CULPEPER, Nicholas, *The Complete Herbal*, 1653

DAVID, Elizabeth, *French Provincial Cooking*, Michael Joseph, 1960

DAVID, Elizabeth, *A Book of Mediterranean Food*, Macdonald, 1958

DAVID, Elizabeth, *Spices, Salt and Aromatics in the English Kitchen*, Penguin, 1970

References

DAY, Harvey, *The Complete Book of Curries*, Kaye and Ward, 1966

DEIGHTON, Len, *Action Cook Book*, Jonathan Cape, 1967

DE MAUDUIT, Vicomte, *They Can't Ration These*, Michael Joseph, 1940

DRUMMOND, J. C., and WILBRAHAM, Anne, *The Englishman's Food*, Jonathan Cape, rev. ed. 1957

EVERARD, Barbara, and MORLEY, Brian D., *Wild Flowers of the World*, Ebury Press, Michael Joseph, 1970

EVELYN, John, *Acetaria*, 1699

FITZGIBBON, Theodora, *The Art of British Cooking*, Phoenix House, 1965

FITZGIBBON, Theodora, *A Taste of Ireland*, Dent, 1968

FLIESS, Walter and Jenny, *Modern Vegetarian Cookery*, Penguin, 1964

GERARD, John, *The Herbal*, 1597

GILES, W. F., 'Our vegetables, whence they came', *Royal Horticultural Society Journal*, Vol 69, 1944

GOOD HOUSEKEEPING INSTITUTE, Cookery Book, 1948

GRIGSON, Geoffrey, *The Englishman's Flora*, Phoenix House, 1958

GODWIN, H., *The History of the British Flora*, Cambridge, 1956

HATFIELD, Audrey Wynne, *How to Enjoy your Weeds*, Muller, 1969

HELBAEK, Hans, 'Studying the diet of ancient man', *Archaeology* 14, 1961

HEMPHILL, Rosemary, *Herbs and Spices*, Penguin, 1966

HENSLOW, G., 'The Origin and History of our Garden Vegetables', *Royal Horticultural Society Journal*, Vols 36, 37, 1910–11

HUTCHINS, Sheila, *English Recipes*, Methuen, 1967

HARTLEY, Dorothy, *Food in England*, Macdonald, 1954

JOHNS, C. A., and BLAKELOCK, R. A., *Flowers of the Field*, Routledge and Kegan Paul, rev. ed. 1949

LANGE, M., and HORA, F. E., *Mushrooms and Toadstools*, Collins, 1963

LEVY, Juliette de Bairacli, *Herbal Handbook for Everyone*, Faber, 1966

LOEWENFELD, Claire, *Fungi*, Faber, 1956

LOEWENFELD, Claire, *Nuts*, Faber, 1957

LOEWENFELD, Claire, and BACK, Philippa, *Herbs for Health and Cookery*, Pan, 1965

MCCLINTOCK, D., and FITTER, R. S. R., *The Pocket Guide to Wild Flowers*, Collins, 1956

MARKHAM, Gervase, *The English Hus-Wife*, 1615

MARTIN, W. KEBLE, *The Concise British Flora in Colour*, Ebury Press, Michael Joseph, 1965

MASEFIELD, G. B., WALLIS, M., HARRISON, S. G., NICHOLSON, B. E., *The Oxford Book of Food Plants*, Oxford, 1969

MEAD, William Edward, *The English Medieval Feast*, Allen and Unwin, 1931

MEDSGER, Oliver Perry, *Edible Wild Plants*, The Macmillan Co, 1966

MILNE-REDHEAD, E. (ed), *The Conservation of the British Flora*, The Botanical Society of the British Isles, 1963

MINISTRY OF AGRICULTURE, *British Poisonous Plants*, H.M.S.O. Bulletin No 161, 1954

MINISTRY OF AGRICULTURE, *Edible and Poisonous Fungi*, H.M.S.O. Bulletin No 43, 1947

MINISTRY OF FOOD, *Hedgerow Harvest*, 1943

NICHOLSON, B. E., and BRIGHTMAN, F. H., *The Oxford Book of Flowerless Plants*, Oxford 1966

NORTH, Pamela, *Poisonous Plants and Fungi*, Blandford, 1967

PENNINGTON, Winifred, *The History of British Vegetation*, EUP, 1969

PERRING, F. (ed), *The Flora of a Changing Britain*, The Botanical Society of the British Isles and E. W. Classey Ltd, 1970

PIRIE, N. W., *Food Resources: Conventional and Novel*, Penguin, 1969

PLINY, *Natural History*, trans W. H. S. Jones, 1951

POLUNIN, Oleg, *Flowers of Europe*, Oxford, 1969

RAMSBOTTOM, J., *Edible Fungi*, Penguin, 1943

RANSON, F., *British Herbs*, Penguin, 1949

RODEN, Claudia, *A Book of Middle Eastern Food*, Nelson, 1968

STEARN, W. T., 'The origin and later development of cultivated plants', *Royal Horticultural Society Journal* Vol 90, July and August 1965

SCOTT, T. H., and STOKOE, W. J., *Wild Flowers of the Wayside and Woodland*, Frederick Warne, 1940

TREASE, George Edward, *A Textbook of Pharmacognosy*, Baillière, Tindall and Cox, 1961

TURNER, William, *The Herbal*, 1568

WALLIS, T. E., *Textbook of Pharmacognosy*, Churchill, 1960

WARNER, *Antiquitates culinariae*, 1791

WHITE, Florence, *Good Things in England*, Jonathan Cape, 1968

VEDEL, H., and LANGE, J., *Trees and Bushes*, Methuen, 1960

ZEITLMAYR, Linus, *Wild Mushrooms*, Muller, 1968

This is in no way a comprehensive list, but an account of the books and papers I referred to most whilst writing this book. I have not listed books from which I have used no more than a single extract in the text. (In most cases I have tried to give the details of the first printing of the most recent English hardback edition of each title, except where the original edition was a paperback.)

Index

Figures in **bold** type refer to plate numbers